Renaissance
into
Baroque

Renaissance into Baroque

Italian Master Drawings
by the Zuccari
1550 ✶ 1600

E. James Mundy

with the assistance of

Elizabeth Ourusoff
de Fernandez-Gimenez

Milwaukee Art Museum
in association with

Cambridge University Press

Cambridge   Melbourne   New York   Port Chester   Sydney

Exhibition Schedule
Milwaukee Art Museum
Milwaukee, Wisconsin
November 17, 1989 - January 14, 1990

National Academy of Design
New York, New York
March 13, 1990 - April 29, 1990

This exhibition was supported in part by grants from the National Endowment for the Arts, a Federal agency and Sotheby's.

Library of Congress Catalogue Card Number: 89-12920
Renaissance into Baroque: Italian Master Drawings by the Zuccari, 1550-1600 by E. James Mundy with the assistance of Elizabeth Ourusoff de Fernandez-Gimenez.

"Exhibition schedule: Milwaukee Art Museum, Milwaukee, Wisconsin, November 17, 1989-January 14, 1990; National Academy of Design, New York, New York, March 13, 1990-April 29, 1990"—T.p. verso.
Includes bibliographical references.
ISBN 0-944110-01-0 (Paper)
ISBN 0-521-39095-8 (Cloth)
1. Zuccari, Taddeo, 1529-1566—Exhibitions. 2. Zuccari, Federico, 1542 or 3-1609—Exhibitions. 3. Mannerism (Art) —Italy-Exhibitions.   I. Mundy, E. James.   II. De Fernandez-Gimenez, Elizabeth Ourusoff, 1933-   III. Milwaukee Art Museum. IV. National Academy of Design (U.S.)
NC257.Z8A4   1989
741.945—dc20   89-12920
                                                                                        CIP

Cover: Taddeo Zuccaro, *Figure of a Youth*, (Detail)
Fogg Art Museum, Harvard University

Designed by J. Eugene Felsch
Printed in the United States of America
by Bulfin Printers, Inc., Milwaukee, Wisconsin
1.5SB/1.55HB/43M

Published by the Press Syndicate of the University of Cambridge
The Pitt Building, Trumpington Street, Cambridge CB2 1RP
40 West 20th Street, New York, NY 10011, USA
10 Stamford Road, Oakleigh, Melbourne 3166, Australia

CONTENTS

LENDERS TO THE EXHIBITION

Ackland Art Museum, University of North Carolina at Chapel Hill

Marcello Aldega/Margot Gordon, New York

Allen Memorial Art Museum, Oberlin College

Art Gallery of Ontario, Toronto

The Art Institute of Chicago

The Art Museum, Princeton University

The Baltimore Museum of Art

Thomas C. Bartee

The Cleveland Museum of Art

Cooper-Hewitt Museum, The Smithsonian Institution's National Institute of Design, New York

Dr. Carlo M. Croce

Mr. and Mrs. R. Fraser Elliott Collection

Duke Roberto Ferretti

Fogg Art Museum, Harvard University, Cambridge, Massachusetts

Helen Getler Fine Art, Roslyn, New York

J. Paul Getty Museum, Malibu

Hill-Stone Inc., New York

Jak Katalan

Rusty Lemorande

Los Angeles County Museum of Art

Mackenzie Art Gallery, Regina, Saskatchewan

The Metropolitan Museum of Art, New York

Alfred Moir

Museum of Fine Arts, Boston

National Gallery of Art, Washington, D.C.

National Gallery of Canada, Ottawa

The Nelson-Atkins Museum of Art, Kansas City

Nissman, Abromson & Co., Brookline

The Philadelphia Museum of Art

The Pierpont Morgan Library, New York

The Rosenbach Museum and Library, Philadelphia

The Saint Louis Art Museum

The Snite Museum of Art, University of Notre Dame

Mrs. A. Alfred Taubman

Mr. and Mrs. David Tobey

University Art Museum, University of California, Santa Barbara

The University of Michigan Museum of Art, Ann Arbor

The Woodner Family Collection

Worcester Art Museum

Yale University Art Gallery, New Haven

Private Collections

FOREWORD

*R*enaissance into Baroque: Italian Master Drawings by the Zuccari, 1550 - 1600 represents a singular moment in the history of the Milwaukee Art Museum. While the museum has organized various exhibitions of earlier painting, this is the first exhibition of old master drawings to be organized by the institution. Further, it is the first exhibition of earlier art organized by the museum to travel. We are grateful to the National Academy of Design and particularly to its Director, John H. Dobkin, for participating with us in this important exhibition.

The significance of this exhibition, both in its scholarly importance and its aesthetic impact, is entirely the result of the efforts of Chief Curator James Mundy. He brought this concept — the first exhibition of the Italian master draughtsmen, Taddeo and Frederico Zuccaro in North America — to the Milwaukee Art Museum upon his arrival here in 1986. Despite a number of other important exhibition projects, he has brought this exhibition and its catalogue to fruition in a manner that sets a very high standard for future endeavors. In addition to creating a catalogue which carefully documents and assesses the more than one hundred drawings in the exhibition, he has obtained the support of Sotheby's and Cambridge University Press in its publication and distribution. We are grateful, too, for their participation.

Renaissance into Baroque: Italian Master Drawings by the Zuccari, while limited to works in North American collections, reflects the broad accomplishment of these two artists as they adapted the styles of Michelangelo and Italian Mannerism into early aspects of the Baroque. The exhibition reveals not only their contribution to draughtmanship but suggests its relationship to their projects in painting and fresco. In short, the drawings of Taddeo and Frederico Zuccaro allow us, as drawings so often do, an intimate view of the conceptual process of the artist, one seen through spontaneous and skillful hands.

Russell Bowman
Director
Milwaukee Art Museum

ACKNOWLEDGMENTS

*R*enaissance into Baroque: Italian Master Drawings by the Zuccari, 1550-1600 is the first examination of the art of the brothers Taddeo (1529-1566) and Federico (1540/41-1609) Zuccaro in North America. It is the first exhibition to be devoted to these very influential Italian masters since the two exhibitions organized by John Gere at the Uffizi in 1966 and the Louvre in 1969 (see bibliography). Unlike those exhibitions which studied the substantial holdings of each institution, the 104 drawings in this exhibition are assembled from a broad range of North American public and private collections. Insuring the success of the project was the tremendous support given by the lenders. Only two loan requests for drawings were turned down, insuring that the very best examples of the work of the two artists could be included. It is the first step on the way to a complete *catalogue raisonné* of the drawings of Federico, a volume which, it is hoped, will complement Mr. Gere's important study of Taddeo's drawings published in 1969.

I am first and foremost grateful to John Gere, retired Keeper of Drawings at the British Museum for his generous support of this project. His kindness and hospitality while sharing with me his many insights into the art of both brothers are particularly appreciated.

This exhibition and its publication would not have been possible without the generous support of the National Endowment for the Arts and Sotheby's. I would like to thank the staffs at both these institutions, particularly Scott Schaefer at Sotheby's, for their assistance at many levels. The cloth edition of the publication is being copublished by the Milwaukee Art Museum and Cambridge University Press. I would like to thank Dr. Beatrice Rehl of Cambridge for her interest in the project.

At the Milwaukee Art Museum many staff members have contributed to make this exhibition a reality. I would like to thank Russell Bowman, director of the art museum, for allowing me to undertake this project in spite of the foreign nature of its subject in regard to the collections and exhibition history of the institution. I have been aided every step of the way by our research assistant, Elizabeth Ourusoff de Fernandez-Gimenez. Her enthusiasm for and extremely valuable contributions to this project cannot be overestimated. While the text of this catalogue and its various shortcomings are mine alone, the unstinting labors of Ms. Fernandez have made a great difference in the quality of this endeavor. Former curatorial assistant Dawn von Wiegand and department secretary Su Molony-Zipter have contributed in various ways. The Art Museum's registrar Leigh Albritton has done a masterful job in co-ordinating the loans. The installation design was planned by John Irion with the whimsical entrance to the show, based on the garden portal to the Palazzo Zuccaro, designed by Melanie Graham. The catalogue was designed by head designer, J. Eugene Felsch.

Friends and colleagues in a number of cities have made distinctive contributions to this exhibition. Dr. and Mrs. Malcolm Bick first stimulated my interest in the drawings of the Zuccari. It is an irony that the important small sketch of *Saint Paul Curing the Paralytic* (see Mundy 1981, pp. 83-85), once in the Bick Collection could not be included in this exhibition. John Varriano and Wendy Watson were generous in sharing their knowledge of Rome and its environs. Information on new drawings and previously known works has been kindly supplied by Julien Stock, Hugo Chapman, Jean-Luc Baroni, Frederik Duparc, John Gere, David McTavish, Michael Moatti, William Johnston, Richard Harprath, Werner Schade, Janos Scholz, Barry Wind and Alfred Moir.

The director of the National Academy of Design, John Dobkin and his staff, particularly curator of prints and drawings, Dita Amory and registrar Barbara Krulick have been exceptionally cooperative. I appreciate greatly their efforts to bring this exhibition before the New York public.

For their assistance in obtaining loans for the exhibition and in the research for this catalogue I would like to thank: Dean Walker, Ackland Art Museum, University of North Carolina at Chapel Hill; Marcello Aldega and Margot Gordon, Rome and New York; Larry Feinberg, Allen Memorial Art Museum, Oberlin College; Katharine Lochnan, Art Gallery of Ontario, Toronto; Charles Stuckey and Suzanne Folds McCullagh, Art Institute of Chicago; Jay Fisher, Baltimore Museum of Art; Nancy Benson; Elisabeth Werdehausen, Matthias Winner and Dieter Graf, Bibliotheca Hertziana, Rome; Michael Miller, The Cleveland Museum of Art; Elaine Evans Dee, Cooper-Hewitt Museum; Aidan Weston Lewis, Witt Library, Courtauld Institute of Art, London; William Robinson and Miriam Stewart, Fogg Art Museum, Harvard University; Helen Sanger and the staff of the Frick Art Reference Library; Helen Getler, Rosalyn, New York; George Goldner, J. Paul Getty Museum; Allan Stone, New York; Bruce Davis, Los Angeles County Museum of Art; Andrew Oko, Mackenzie Art

Gallery, University of Regina, Saskatchewan; Jacob Bean and William Griswold, Metropolitan Museum of Art, New York; Lawrence Kanter, Lehman Collection, Metropolitan Museum of Art, New York; Clifford Ackley and Susan Reed, Museum of Fine Arts, Boston; Andrew Robison and Diane DeGrazia, National Gallery of Art, Washington, D.C.; Mary Cazort, National Gallery of Canada; Roger Ward and George McKenna, Nelson-Atkins Museum of Art, Kansas City; Joan Nissman and Morton Abromson, Brookline; Ann Percy and Carmen Bambach-Cappel, Philadelphia Art Museum; Charles Pierce, Cara Dennison and David Wright, Pierpont Morgan Library, New York; Kimerly Rorschach, The Rosenbach Museum and Library; Judith Weiss-Levy, Saint Louis Art Museum; Stephen Spiro, Snite Museum of Art, University of Notre Dame; Allen Rosenbaum and Barbara Ross, The Art Museum, Princeton University; Jennifer Jones and Kristen Zaremba, Woodner Family Collection; David Farmer, University Art Museum Santa Barbara; Graham Smith and Hilarie Faberman, University of Michigan Museum of Art, Ann Arbor; David Acton, Worcester Art Museum; Richard Field and Susan Frankenbach, Yale University Art Gallery; and the departments of Interlibrary Loans and Special Collections at the Golda Meir Library, University of Wisconsin, Milwaukee. I would also like to thank those private collectors who thought enough of the idea of this exhibition to part with a number of valuable works of art for a six-month period.

Finally, I would like to acknowledge the substantial contribution made to this project by my wife, Kelli Peduzzi. It is to her that this publication is affectionately dedicated.

E. James Mundy
Chief Curator
Milwaukee Art Museum

BETWEEN RENAISSANCE AND BAROQUE: TADDEO AND FEDERICO ZUCCARO

By E. James Mundy

The historical analogy which assumes that the "dawn" of a new age must be preceded by relative "darkness" has been all too often employed when considering the period 1550-1600. It is a tidy system but not always an accurate one.

Taddeo and Federico Zuccaro belong to a group of late sixteenth-century Italian artists, among them Perino del Vaga, Polidoro da Caravaggio, Francesco Salviati, Giorgio Vasari, Jacopo Bertoia, Cesare Nebbia and Jacopo Zucchi, who played dominant roles in the visual culture of central Italy but whose works and achievements are little known to us now. It was these artists who fulfilled the most important artistic commissions during a period of great activity generated by, among other patrons, Popes Paul III (1534-49), Pius IV (1559-65), Gregory XIII (1572-85), and Sixtus V (1585-90).

One reason for our general lack of knowledge of these artists is, in part, temporal and intellectual. The artists who inhabited Italy in the last half of the sixteenth century when the Zuccari were creating their most important work were in the uncomfortable position of following in the artistic footsteps of Michelangelo, Raphael and Titian, whose achievements were models for the resurgence of painting after the Sack of Rome in 1527. For example, no artist could ignore the Sistine Chapel, recently decorated by Michelangelo, when conceiving of a new decorative fresco project. It was expected by patron and artist alike that such previous accomplishments could be attained once more. The great decorative projects of the High Renaissance gave hope for renewal after the political situation had calmed down and capital as well as artists began returning to Rome. While the opportunities for distinction existed for this generation of artists, the inevitable comparison with the great masters of the age was always part of their artistic *milieu* and critical legacy. For the next four centuries the critical and art historical apparatus would seem to hold this generation accountable for not rivaling their great forefathers. This judgment was harsher exactly because these artists tried so hard to walk the path prescribed by Raphael and Michelangelo. Therefore, art historians would, in

13

turn, devote more time and energy to the likes of the Carracci, Caravaggio, Bernini, and Borromini, completely "Baroque" painters, sculptors and architects of the following generation who drastically re-channeled artistic expectations, and spend less energy on that group who continued to contribute to the evolution of the Renaissance.

A second reason is physical. The paintings of these artists were primarily large scale fresco commissions for palaces and churches. Thus, they are immovable and cannot be seen in the great art museums of Europe and the Americas, conveniently labeled for the visitor. Many are virtually inaccessible to the visitor in Rome or other cities due to private ownership or highly restricted, or non-existent hours of visitation, while others, still, are in remote villas, quiet churches and lonely palaces that only the tireless and dedicated enthusiast would be likely to pursue.

Thus, the best way for most of us to get to know these artists is through their drawings. Even this can be something of a difficult process since most are not often on view and the student must frequently make special arrangements to view them.

Hence, an exhibition such as this one, of over one hundred drawings by the Zuccari, provides the rare opportunity of confronting the development of these two artists' styles against the historical backdrop of a fifty year period of evolution. Bringing them together condenses years of a specialist's energetic searching into a small portion of the day for the visitor.

The half century spanned by the drawings in this exhibition is one that moves from the self-sustaining virtuosity of the last years of Italian Mannerism, where inversion of the natural and expected relations of things was the norm, to the programmatic religious zeal and bombast found at the height of the Counter Reformation. Taddeo Zuccaro (1529-1566), in his brief but intense eighteen-year career as an artist, took the visual vocabulary of Mannerism and, in a sense escorted the movement, to its ultimate demise. By the time of his death, Italian art, in part thanks to the emphasis on clear, religious messages meant to stir the spirit, would be ready to leave behind the obscurities and intentional artifice, that were the priorities of Mannerism. Taddeo's sole arena was the Roman artistic world. His younger brother Federico (1540/41-1609) would use his brother's model to educate himself as an artist, but would, during a fifty-year career, reflect the almost missionary zeal and relentless spiritual pragmatism of official art after the last Council of Trent in 1563, that cemented the artistic goals of the Counter Reformation. Federico's art would suggest the worldliness of the artist/gentleman welcome at the courts of several Popes, English and Spanish royalty as well as the Venetian patriarchy. The intensity of a pure regional style in Taddeo's work, steeped in the examples of Raphael, Michelangelo and Polidoro da Caravaggio and fostered by the prevailing religious and humanist needs of Roman sponsors, would ultimately yield to the common denominator of Federico's achievement, that drew on many different artistic traditions. While Taddeo might be said to revel in the local artistic dialect, Federico would aspire, in his drawing, painting and his theoretical works, to a visual form of *Esperanto*. Federico's need to satisfy his patrons' expectations might have had an impact on his style, encouraging a more homogeneous manner of portrayal that was equally at home in Rome, Venice or Madrid. Taddeo, on the other hand, seemed to choose his own course and stick to it during his brief career, striving to equal the grandeur and expressiveness of the late work of Raphael and Michelangelo.

There is a captivating purity found in the robust painting and drawing of Taddeo and in the artist's own self-effacing presence as an historical entity. In most respects, his personality was eclipsed by his work as an artist. The romance and travails of his early career were celebrated in the series of twenty-four allegorical and narrative scenes executed in the 1590's by Federico (see cat. no. 96). His early biographies, written by Vasari and Baglione, reveal little about the artist as person aside from what was a driving need to take on more and more projects. From all accounts, he got along well with others in the artistic community, was obviously well regarded by powerful patrons, and lived entirely for his art to the point of occasionally taking on more than it was reasonable to believe that he could finish. The details of his artistic output and the interpretive history of the artist have been thoroughly studied by John Gere in a series of important articles, books and exhibition catalogues between 1963-70 (see bibliography). Taddeo's earliest works are redolent of the manner of Polidoro da Caravaggio and the late works of Raphael (see cat. nos. 1-8) as he submerged himself in the style and artistic vocabulary of the most Roman of Roman art. It is at this moment, around the year 1550, that he worked primarily on palace façades and interior decorative schemes, imbuing these projects with a subdued sense of physical power and working toward the ability of achieving a sculptural feeling in his drawings and paintings.

What would follow would be a period of intense activity highlighted by two major religious commissions, the series of frescoes in the small Mattei Chapel in the Roman church of S. Maria della Consolazione between 1553-56 and larger decorations for the Frangipani Chapel, also in Rome, in S. Marcello al Corso started around 1557 but left unfinished at his death in 1566 (see cat. nos. 11-21).

started around 1557 but left unfinished at his death in 1566 (see cat. nos. 11-21). These two commissions demonstrate the dominant effect that Michelangelo's art would begin to exert on Taddeo, particularly his frescoes in the Pauline Chapel. The bold pre-eminence given to the human form would serve as the impulse to Taddeo's creativity in the late 50s and early 60s.

The three years prior to Taddeo's death were also remarkably productive and he created his most vibrant and balanced art at this time. His synthesis of Roman art traditions and his ability to invent many new variations on existing narrative or compositional themes now took place. At the end of 1563, Taddeo assumed the completion of the decorations for the Sala dei Fasti Farnesiani in the Palazzo Farnese following the death of Francesco Salviati (see cat. no. 34-37). There followed shortly thereafter the important papal commission to paint portions of the Sala Regia at the Vatican for which he received his first payment on 4 May 1564 (see cat. nos. 31-32).

These commissions would set the stage for the *summa* of Taddeo's powers of expression and compositional organization, achieved in the ambitious and spectacular decoration of the Farnese country villa at Caprarola which we can assume was begun as early as 1561 and continued after Taddeo's death by Federico and other artists (see cat. nos. 38-42). As one moves through the palace today the audacity of the program and its cumulative power on the viewer is as freshly felt as in the sixteenth century. The bold translation of the Farnese family's history into mythology are largely the result of Taddeo's uncompromising vision and interpretation of the iconographical program set out by Cardinal Alessandro Farnese, and a small circle of humanist scholars including Paolo Manuzio, Onofrio Panvinio and Annibale Caro. The result is an architectural and painterly *Gesamtkunstwerk* with decidedly humanist underpinnings.

Taddeo's early drawing style is almost a sculptural process. By concentrating on the tradition of Roman façade decoration, itself derived from ancient Roman relief sculpture, Taddeo developed a mode of drawing in pen, brush and ink with wash, or chalk that seemed to prepare him in the late 1550's for the reception of Michelangelo's own sculptural drawing manner. The highly mannered poses and almost unnatural, but ultimately believable, physical abilities of some figures in Taddeo's frescoes in the Frangipani Chapel and Caprarola are the dividends of this style of drawing so influenced by a sculptural sensibility. The ability to understand the three dimensional implications of a two dimensional process is present in the artist's earliest works on paper where he begins to explore and understand the play of light across a body or object.

While at the height of his powers as a draughtsman between 1558-1566, the manner in which Taddeo used line becomes particularly exciting, electric and distinctive. A survey of some of the works in this catalogue (nos. 13, 22, 26, 27 and 38, for example) provide the viewer with the essential visual characteristics that distinguish Taddeo from his peers, particularly the way he delineates a figure in pen sometimes without a seeming beginning or end. These figures often appear to have been sculpted in wire. Given Taddeo's shorter career and the fewer influences on him than on Federico, the stylistic progression and personality of his work is more compressed and linear than that of other, longer lived artists, including his brother. Perhaps, therefore, his artistic development can be more easily understood.

However, because the career of Federico Zuccaro was longer than that of his brother and he was subjected to more diverse influences, his work as a draughtsman is, in many respects, less well understood. He has not been the subject of monographic studies. However, some excellent work, for example the articles by Heikamp, Körte and Hermann-Fiore (see bibliography), has concentrated on the esoteric aspects of his iconography and theoretical ambitions. What actually makes up the graphic work of Federico, and how it relates to his overall development as an artist, is still a jumble of hundreds of drawings and sketches that have had fluid attributions ranging from Taddeo to shadowy and anonymous members of the "workshop". This exhibition may be a first step to putting the *oeuvre* of the artist in order.

Federico Zuccaro was brought to Rome in 1550, at the early age of around ten, to live and learn from his brother. It is predictable that his early drawings would reflect his brother's style and that there would be some difficulty, at times, distinguishing between the two artists during the years 1555-63 when they are working closely together. This is particularly the case with the drawings for Caprarola and the Pucci Chapel of S. Trinità dei Monti in Rome (see cat. nos. 38-46). Here we see Federico in his most Taddean moments. Vasari indicates that Taddeo looked out for his brother's early professional interests and that his efforts to improve on Federico's work could occasionally create friction between them as in the case of his decorations of the façade of the house of Tizio da Spoleto with moments from the life of Saint Eustace, when, around 1558, after Taddeo retouched some of his painting, he reportedly fell into a rage and destroyed a work of art by his brother (Vasari 1850, V, pp.192-93, also see cat. no.

48).

In 1563, after having gained the attention of patrons for his participation in some of Taddeo's larger projects, Federico was called away from Rome for the first time to execute several commissions for Cardinal Grimani in Venice. Thus began regular travels for the artist that took him away from Rome to Florence, Orvieto, Madrid, Valencia, London, Antwerp, Nancy, back to Venice, Loreto, Lucca, Pavia, Mantua, Parma and Ancona over the course of the next forty-five years. With each journey, Federico would exhale into a foreign atmosphere some of the breath of Taddeo's art and the late *maniera* of Rome. His paintings for the Grimani Chapel in 1564 (see cat. no. 52-53), the Orvieto Cathedral in 1568 (see cat. no. 58), and the Sala del Gran Consiglio in the Ducal Palace, Venice in the 1580s (see. cat. nos. 86-88) are such examples. At the same time he would inhale a range of different styles and adjust to constantly shifting expectations of different patrons and publics. Whereas it would be fair to say that Taddeo's style was invented in Rome, Federico's was forged in an international crucible. He was not, however, a courtly artistic chameleon, reflecting whatever style or subject happened to be in favor. He seemed to make the best possible use of the examples of other artists, attempting to incorporate the special qualities of a Titian, Barocci, Michelangelo, or even Holbein with his solid Roman training.

The wide stylistic range of his drawings might be expected but it still, at times, surprises the viewer. A drawing such as no. 48, *The Vision of Saint Eustace* when viewed beside no. 99, his study for *The Canonization of Saint Hyacinth* presents an excellent opportunity to appreciate the scope of the problem in successfully assembling the artist's drawings and articulating any cogent development. How, then, does the sculptural and corporeal presence of the former evolve into the spidery linearism and shorthand description of the latter?

The influence of the Counter-Reformation on the two brothers also becomes a point of substantial contrast. Taddeo's active career paralleled the important moments of decision that took place at Trent between 1545-63. The effects on art of the Ecumenical Council's deliberations in the final year, attempting to tame the obscurities and intentionally impenetrable meaning of the Mannerist era by expressing a strong propagandistic content of redemption couched in a clarity and correctness of portrayal of religious narrative, did not have a particularly strong effect on Taddeo's work. Certainly the work in the Mattei Chapel conveys none of the simplicity, realism or emotional stimulus to piety that arose as the paramount requirements of religious art. While one can search for, and find, a greater degree of these details in the Frangipani chapel decorations, Taddeo continued to engage in the depiction of superhuman characters acting out fundamentally dramatic yet sublime and frightening moments of revelation, punishment, or miraculous intervention. Even the work for the Farnese in both Rome and Caprarola does not seem much affected by the recent acts of reform. He was, essentially, impervious to the effects of the Council of Trent's decisions. One might, however, begin to see a few of the effects of Post-Tridentine imagery in the decorations for the Pucci Chapel, particularly in the portions completed by Federico by 1589. How the art of Taddeo might have been altered by the zealous application of Counter Reformation artistic principles is an interesting question to ponder. Would he have been able, or have wanted, to alter his personal vision and adapt to the changing artistic climate by 1580 as Federico seemed able to do? Would these pressures have yielded an entirely different artistic response in Taddeo's art?

The effect of the rulings of the last Council of Trent can be seen much more clearly in Federico's art, particularly that executed between 1580 and 1609. His dismissal from the Caprarola decorations in 1569, owing to a desultory commitment to its completion, marks as well the start of his distancing of himself from the art of his brother. Not having his brother's example to guide, and at times, to contend with, would substantially alter his art. His travels during the 1570's and 80's ending with his presence in Spain between 1585-88 would draw him gradually into line with the ideals of clarity, realism and devotional stimulation. Thus, the work in the Casa Santa at Loreto in 1583, the paintings for the high altar of San Lorenzo at the Escorial near Madrid in 1585-88, the Capella degli Angeli in the Gesú, Rome, the center of Counter Reformation thought and imagery, in 1592 and the Saint Hyacinth Chapel in S. Sabina, Rome in 1600 represent a steadily increasing consonance between the propagandistic aims of the Catholic church and Federico's ability, certainly borne of pragmatism, to satisfy his patron's wishes. Then as now, institutions could have a dramatic effect on what art was and how it appeared. It can be maintained that the antidote for this regimen of Roman Catholic clarity of purpose was to be found in the decorations of his private residences in Florence and Rome, where the occasional elegant caprices of the increasingly learned artist could find their proper *metier* (see cat. nos. 78 and 96).

The characteristic in the work of the two brothers that serves best to separate their different views of art, or conceivably, how art in general changed between the death of Taddeo in 1566 and Federico in 1609, is their approach to what art can be used to signify. For Taddeo, the human body was the primary conveyance of meaning, metaphorical or actual. His compositions are often titanic corporeal proving grounds for basic ideas regarding spirituality or history. For him, general visual statements were, often, enough.

For Federico, the rarified symbols that denoted learning and the arcane visual language of the gentleman often predominated in his art. His allegorical compositions, *The Lament of Painting*, *Porta Virtutis* (cat. no. 85), or *Calumny of Apelles*, all reflect a desire on the part of the artist to explore arcane visual references to humanist learning. Yet, when this language was decoded, it carried a specific meaning that spoke to a sophisticated, educated audience. Equally so, when contriving his larger religious works, the messages again tend to be quite specific in executing the wishes of a clergy that after the last Council of Trent, had an explicit program for the artist to follow.

In the art of both brothers the viewer can expect to find the occasional drastic change of approach when the function of the work of art itself changed. For example, Taddeo worked on chapel decorations, palace frescoes, altarpieces and even designs for the famous "Spanish" maiolica service given to Philip II of Spain by Guidobaldo II della Rovere, Duke of Urbino in 1562 (see cat. no. 29 and Gere 1963). In 1559, he quickly designed thirteen paintings, trophies and other ornaments for the obsequies of Emperor Charles V in S. Giacomo di Spagnuoli (see Berendson 1970). With each of these different types of conception, the general approach of the artist to the idea tended to change somewhat.

Federico was also involved in major palace and religious decorative schemes as well as altarpieces. There is no evidence that he composed designs for maiolica workshops like his brother, but he did create specialized designs for printmakers and festivals, such as the great canvas backdrop depicting an elaborate hunt designed to help celebrate the arrival of Queen Joanna of Austria in Florence on 15 December 1565.

Unlike his brother who never seems to have painted or drawn portrait likenesses, Federico frequently portrayed friends and family in his sketches (see for example cat. nos. 72, 73, 76 and 97) and painted famous patrons such as Elizabeth I and the Earl of Leicester in England. His career, again unlike that of his brother, strove toward a high degree of self-aggrandizement as well as self-portrayal. Aside from painting or drawing himself on several occasions, Federico also had commemorative medals struck in his own honor in 1578 and 1588, an act not uncommon to nobles but rather foreign to artists.

In Federico's case, a sense of self-importance would also yield more frequent moments of conflict with patrons and other artists. His public battle with the

Bolognese artistic establishment ending with his banishment from Rome by the Bolognese Pope Gregory XIII (see cat. no. 85), the famous petty and curmudgeonly annotations in his personal copy of Vasari's *Vite*, now in the Uffizi, and his financial over-extension arising from his elaborate plans for his Roman palace suggest an artist with a strong will, combative personality and an exaggerated sense of his own worth. Curiously, this very clear impression of Federico's personality, when considered against the virtual lack of a distinct impression of Taddeo as a person, contributed to an unsympathetic audience for his art in later centuries. His apparently acrimonious envy of Giorgio Vasari would turn nineteenth-century writers like Bottari and Mrs. Foster away from Federico, singling him out as a "false friend and malignant detractor" (Vasari 1850 V, p. 200, footnote). Certainly, something of this Victorian antipathy toward an adversary of Vasari has continued in some of the modern criticism of Federico. Gere's treatment of Federico's role in the history of art is rather severe throughout his writings.

Federico was not able to improve on his brother's artistic achievement and, unquestionably, attempted to compensate for it in other ways including the adoption of social pretensions one never finds in Taddeo's behavior. Federico's art does, nonetheless, occupy a position of importance in the history of art. He carried his brother's artistic legacy with him throughout his travels. He became something of a role model for the proliferation of courtier/artists during the next two centuries. And, finally, he contributed substantially to the increasing codification of creating art in his theoretical writings and academic procedures in the training of artists.

Seeing the drawings of Taddeo and Federico Zuccaro together sharpens our ability to recognize the evolution of one artist's style into another and one period style into a second. In Taddeo's drawings one can clearly detect the sounds of the last movement of a Roman symphony composed by Raphael and Michelangelo. These melodies grow fainter in Federico's work, yielding somewhat to a growing external demand for a return to rationality as the influence of his brother subsides during the Counter Reformation. The full realization of high levels of expression blended with a clearly defined religious or political purpose in art would be achieved shortly after Federico's death in 1609 and would define what has been called the "triumph" of the Baroque age.

At times, in assessing the development of Taddeo and Federico Zuccaro's art, it is difficult to decide if the process is one of evolution or mutation. The degree of artistic attraction and filial admiration for Taddeo's achievement that Federico would continue to evidence would also become something of a liability as time went on. And it can be concluded that in the end, the growing uniformity of artistic style would conquer in Federico's art over Taddeo's individualism. This internal victory would grow simultaneously with the development of the Academy as it set the rules for much Baroque painting. As such Federico Zuccaro becomes an important link in the span between Renaissance and Baroque.

COLOR PLATES

6. Taddeo Zuccaro, *Scene from Roman History*, Private Collection

11. Taddeo Zuccaro, *Study of a Man seen from Behind*, c. 1553-56,
The National Gallery of Art, Washington, D.C.

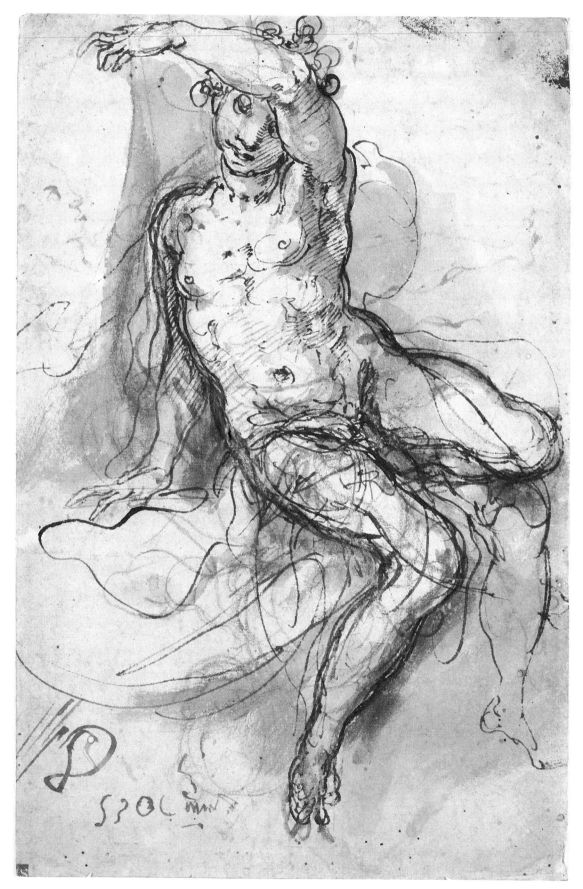

13. Taddeo Zuccaro, *Figure of a Youth*, Fogg Art Museum, Harvard University, Cambridge

14. Taddeo Zuccaro, *Sheet of Studies for the Blinding of Elymas, Sacrifice at Lystra, and a Holy Family*, Art Institute of Chicago

16. Taddeo Zuccaro, *St. Paul Restoring Eutychus to Life*, c. 1557-58, The Metropolitan Museum of Art, New York

22. Taddeo Zuccaro, *St. John the Baptist Preaching*, The Pierpont Morgan Library, New York

30　23. Taddeo Zuccaro, *Temperance*, c. 1556-62, National
Gallery of Canada, Ottawa

26. Taddeo Zuccaro, *Women Approaching a Small Image of a Bull*, c. 1560, The Pierpont Morgan Library, New York

27. Taddeo Zuccaro, *Studies for a Circular Composition of Diana and her Nymphs Bathing*, c. 1560, The Metropolitan Museum of Art, New York

35. Taddeo Zuccaro, *A Group of Warriors*, c. 1563-65, The Pierpont Morgan Library, New York

36. Taddeo Zuccaro, *Cardinal Albornoz Giving the Keys of Valentano to the Farnese*, c. 1563-65, The J. Paul Getty Museum, Malibu

38. Taddeo Zuccaro, *Julius III Restoring the Duchy of Parma to Ottavio Farnese*, 1562-63, The Pierpont Morgan Library, New York

41. Federico Zuccaro, *The Lord Creating the Sun and the Moon*, c. 1566, Allen Memorial Art Museum, Oberlin

48. Federico Zuccaro, *The Vision of St. Eustace*, c. 1558-9, The
Metropolitan Museum of Art, New York

55. Federico Zuccaro, *The Holy Trinity and Four Angels*, Otis Norcross Fund Courtesy, Museum of Fine Arts, Boston

56. Federico Zuccaro, *Dead Christ Supported by Angels*, c. 1563, Yale University Art Gallery, New Haven

60. Federico Zuccaro, *Coronation of the Virgin*, c. 1570, Private Collection

62. Federico Zuccaro, *Angels and Putti in the Clouds*, National Gallery of Art, Washington, D.C.

64. Federico Zuccaro, *Disputation of St. Catherine of Alexandria*, c. 1570, National Gallery of Art, Washington, D.C.

66. Federico Zuccaro, *Study for a Scene from the Last Judgment*, c. 1576-79, The Metropolitan Museum of Art, New York

71. Federico Zuccaro, *St. Romuald*, c. 1576-79, The Woodner Family
Collection, New York

77. Federico Zuccaro, *Lady putting on her stockings*, c. 1575-82, The Nelson-Atkins Museum of Art, Kansas City

85. Federico Zuccaro, *Porta Virtutis*, 1582, The Pierpont Morgan Library, New York

87. Federico Zuccaro, *The Submission of the Emperor Frederick Barbarossa to Pope Alexander III*, The J. Paul Getty Museum, Malibu

TADDEO ZUCCARO - CHRONOLOGY

1529	Born at S. Angelo in Vado (Marches)
1543/44	Goes to Rome. Copies antique monuments and works by Polidoro da Caravaggio, Raphael, Michelangelo.
1545	Under his master Danielle Porri da Parma, paints in S. Maria di Alvito in the Abruzzi.
1548	Façade paintings of Furius Camillus for Palazzo Jacopo Mattei, Rome.
1548- c. 1551	Four scenes from life of St. Ambrose for Church of S. Ambrogio (lost); façade paintings of life of Alexander the Great (lost) near S. Lucia della Tinta (cf. cat. no. 7); stories of Mercury on façade of Mattiuolo house (lost); other unidentified façades (cf. cat. nos. 1-3, 5-6).
1550	Temporary decorations (lost) for coronation of Pope Julius III. Probably begins collaboration with Bartolomeo Passarotti (1529-92) who makes etchings based on Taddeo's drawings. (cat. no. 8).
1551	*Occasion and Fortune* (device of Julius III) for one of the Pope's villas (lost).
	Summoned to Urbino by Duke Guidobaldo II to complete decoration of Cathedral choir with scenes from the life of the Virgin.
1552	Goes to Verona with the Duke. Makes copy (lost) of Raphael's *La Perla*; paints portrait of Duke, an unfinished *Conversion of St. Paul*. Decorations for ducal palace in Pesaro.

April 1553- March 1555	Works with Prospero Fontana (1512-1597) decorating Pope Julius III's Villa Giulia with mythological scenes and triumphs.
1553-56	Scenes of the *Passion of Christ* for Mattei Chapel in S. Maria della Consolazione, Rome (cat. nos. 10-12).
1555-56	Paid for work in the Vatican Belvedere for Julius III; for work in Torre di Niccolo V for Pius IV.
c. 1556	Pietà between Saints Peter and Paul, Church of the Pazzarelli, Piazza Colonna (with Federico; lost).
1558	Paid for a drawing of the Madonna for a small altarpiece in the Sistine Chapel.
1558-59	*Flight into Egypt* and *Nativity* for S. Maria dell' Orto.
1558/59- 1566	Frescoes in the Frangipani Chapel, S. Marcello al Corso, Rome (cat. nos. 15-21).
1559	Decorations (lost) for obsequies of Charles V in S. Giacomo di Spagnuoli (assisted by Federico). Frescoes, stucco designs and allegorical figures of *Active* and *Contemplative* life (lost) for a chapel in Orvieto Cathedral. *Christ in Glory with Saints* in apse of S. Sabina, Rome. *Muses on Mount Parnassus* in casino of Palazzo Bufalo (cf. cat. no. 47).
1559-60	Scenes from the life of Alexander the Great at the Castello Orsini-Odescalchi, Bracciano and at the Palazzo Mattei-Caetani, Rome (assisted by Federico).

1560	Scenes of the Passion (with Federico) in Oratory of S. Orsola, S. Giovanni dei Fiorentini (lost).
	Paid for restoration of Raphael's *Apostles* in Sala dei Palafrenieri, Vatican and for work (with Federico) in Aracoeli palace.
	Portrait of Virginia della Rovere (lost).
1560-62	Designs set of maiolica commissioned by the Duke of Urbino for the King of Spain (cf. cat. no. 29).
	Ground floor decoration of Cardinal Alessandro Farnese's villa at Caprarola (cat. no. 39).
Nov. 1562	Receives Antonio Caro's program for decoration of *Stanza di Aurora*, Villa Farnese, Caprarola.
c.1562-63	Decoration of Sala dei Fatti Farnesiani and Anticamera del Concilio, at the Villa Farnese, Caprarola.
1563	Contracts to decorate lower part of North transept of Pucci Chapel in S. Trinità dei Monti (cat. no. 44).
1563-65	Completes decoration of the Sala dei Fasti Farnesiani begun by Salviati for Cardinal Ranuccio Farnese in the Farnese Palace, Rome (cat. nos. 34-37).
1564-65	*Donation of Charlemagne*, *Battle of Tunis*, and *Overdoor* for the Sala Regia of the Vatican (cat. nos. 31-33).
1564	Goes to Florence. Completes Stanza dei Lanefici, Caprarola.
May 1565	Receives iconographic program for Stanza della Solitudine, Caprarola.
Dec. 1565	Stanza della Solitudine at Caprarola probably completed.

c. 1566   Figures of *Prophets* for S. Eligio degli Orefici, Rome (cat. no. 30).

1566   Continues work on Pucci Chapel. Commissioned to paint altarpiece of S. Lorenzo in Damaso.

       Dies September 2nd in Rome.

FEDERICO ZUCCARO - CHRONOLOGY

1540/41	Born at Sant'Angelo in Vado (Marches).
1550	Brought to Rome to live with his brother Taddeo.
1555-60	Assists Taddeo with façades, with Mattei-Caetani and Castello Orsini (Bracciano) commissions, obsequies of Charles V, Pazzarelli *Pietà*, at S. Giovanni dei Fiorentini, and at Vatican.
1558-59	*Annuciation* (paid for June 1561), *Marriage of the Virgin* and *Visitation*, S. Maria dell'Orto. *Parnassus with Muses* in vault of house of Stefano Margani, Rome (lost) (cf. cat no. 47). *Conversion*, *Baptism*, and *Martyrdom* of St. Eustace on Tizio da Spoleto's façade, Piazza Sant'Eustachio, Rome (cat. no. 48). Three scenes from life of St. Paul, S. Maria, Orvieto.
1560	Ground floor decorations of Vatican Loggia (apartments of Innocent VIII) for visit of Cosimo de' Medici and Eleanore of Toledo.
1561-63	Paid for work at the Vatican: *Transfiguration, Marriage at Cana* and other scenes from life of Christ, Casino of Pius IV (cf. cat. no. 23); *Escutcheon of Pius IV flanked by Justice and Equity*, 1562, Ruota Romana; sixteen scenes from the life of Moses, Belvedere, 1563 (cat. no. 49). Assists Taddeo at the Villa Farnese, Caprarola.
Nov. 1563	Summoned to Venice by Cardinal Grimani.

1563-64	*Distributive Justice* (lost, engraved by C. Cort) for Palazzo Grimani. *Adoration of the Magi* (oil), *Resurrection of Lazarus* and *Conversion of the Magdalen* (lost; cat. nos. 52-53), Grimani Chapel, S. Francesco della Vigna. Roman history scenes (lost) for G.B. Pellegrini's villa.
June 1564	Enters competition (won by Tintoretto) for ceiling decoration of Scuola di San Rocco. Paints twelve large scenes for the *Tragedy of King Hyrcanus of Jerusalem* produced by the Scuola della Caza. Travels with Palladio to Cividale del Friuli, Verona and other Lombard cities.
1564-66	Negotiates unsuccessfully for commission to decorate end wall of Sala del Gran Consiglio in Ducal Palace, Venice. Makes drawings and painting (lost) for a large *Paradise* (cat. no. 57).
1565	Allegorical figures for vault of Stanza della Solitudine at Caprarola.
	Admitted to Academy of Drawing in Florence. Hunting scene backdrop for festivities in Florence celebrating the marriage of Francesco de'Medici and Joanna of Austria on Dec. 26, 1565. Inscription on *modello* (Uffizi) gives artist's age as 25 in 1565.
1566	In Rome. *St. Peter in Prison* for the Duke of Urbino (cf. cat. no. 80). Sends a *Virgin in Heaven Surrounded by Angels* to Milan and a figure of Chance to Perugia.
1566-67	Ceilings of the Sala de Gloria and Sala della Fama Villa d'Este, Tivoli, for Ippolito II d'Este, Cardinal of Ferrara. *Henry IV before Gregory VII*, Sala Regia, Vatican. Lunette of *Annuciation* and *Six Prophets with God, Holy Spirit and Angels Above*, S. Maria Annunziata, Rome (destroyed; cat. no. 62).
	Two *quadri riportati* in the Sala dei Fasti Farnesiani, Palazzo Farnese, Rome.

1566-68	Directs decoration of Villa Farnese, Caprarola. Paints chapel and certain frescoes in the Sala d'Ercole (cat. nos. 41, 42).
1566-89	Completes Pucci Chapel begun by Taddeo (cat. nos. 45, 46).
c. 1568-70	Executes Taddeo's commission for S. Lorenzo in Damaso, altarpiece: *Coronation of the Virgin with SS, Lawrence, Paul, Peter, and Damasus* (cat. nos. 60, 61).
c. 1568/69	*Lament of Painting* (lost; engraved by C. Cort).
1568-70	*Christ Healing Blind Man* and *Christ Raising the Son of the Widow of Nain*, (cat. no. 58), Cathedral, Orvieto.
July 1569	Resigns from position at Caprarola.
1569	*The Calumny of Apelles* (Hampton Court, London; engraved by C. Cort, 1572). Lost *Adoration of Magi* for S. Eligio degli Orefici (?), engraved by Jacob Matham.
1570-73	*Conversion of the Empress Faustina*; *Disputation of St. Catherine* (cat. nos.63, 64), *Christ Among the Money Changers*, and *Ecce Homo*, S. Caterina dei Funari, Rome.
1572	Sibyls and Prophets in chapel of Villa d'Este, Tivoli
1573	*Flagellation of Christ, Prophets and Sibyls*, Oratorio del Gonfalone, Rome (cat. no 65).
1574	Travels to France and Netherlands. Works for Cardinal of Lorraine.
March- Oct. 1575	In England. Portraits of Queen Elizabeth I and Earl of Leicester. Copies Holbein frescoes in Steelyard Guild, London.
1575-79	In Florence completes *Last Judgment* begun by Vasari in the

cupola of the Cathedral of S. Maria dei Fiore (cat. nos. 66-71). Becomes member of the Accademia del Disegno. *Annunciation*, S. Maria Nuova.

1576-77   Sketching excursions to Vallombrosa (cat. nos. 71, 74).

1577   Buys house and studio in via Capponi.
             Self-portrait with Vincenzo Borghini (Rome, Bibliotheca Hertziana).

1577-79   Decorates Florentine house and studio with allegorical frescoes of time and seasons, myths and fables (cf. cat. nos. 78, 79).

1578   Has self-commemorative medal struck by Pastorino of Siena.

1580   *The Baptism of Cornelius*, (wall fresco) and vault paintings begun, Cappella Paolina, Vatican (cf. cat. no. 81).

1580-84   *Vision of St. Gregory* (completed 1580) and *Procession of St. Gregory* (lost; engraved by A. Caprioli) for the Ghiselli Chapel at S. Maria del Baraccano, Bologna, criticized and rejected.

1581   Expelled from Rome by Pope Gregory XIII for exhibiting satirical *Porta Virtutis* (lost; cat. no. 85).

1582   Begins *Frederick Barbarossa Submitting to Pope Alexander III* (completed in 1603) for the Sala del Gran Consiglio in the Ducal Palace, Venice (cat. nos. 86-90).

1582-83   *Marriage*, *Visitation* (dated 1583), *Death*, *Coronation*, and *Perpetual Glory of the Virgin Mary* in Casa Santa of Loreto, for Duke of Urbino.

1583-84   Pardoned by Pope, returns to Rome to complete work in the Cappella Paolina: *Arms of Gregory III*, *Pentecost*, *Mission of the Apostles*.

1585	*Christ in Limbo* (Brera, Milan).
1585-1588	For Phillip II of Spain, paints high altar, flanking reliquary altars and frescoes in cloister of the Evangelists, S. Lorenzo, El Escorial.
1587-88	Drawings of Dante's *Divine Comedy* (Uffizi).
1588	Has own portrait medal struck in Spain.
1590-91	Builds Palazzo Zuccaro (now Bibliotheca Hertziana) on Pincian Hill in Rome (cf. cat. no. 98). Granted Roman citizenship for self and descendants.
1592	Vault and altarpiece of Cappella degli Angeli Il Gesù, Rome, commissioned by Vittori family (cat. no. 94).
1593	Becomes first president of reorganized Accademia di S. Luca.
1593-1600	Decoration of Palazzo Zuccaro (cat. no. 96, cf. cat. no. 78).
1594	*Adoration of the Magi*, Cathedral, Lucca.
c. 1594-95	*Christ Bearing the Cross*, Cappella Olgiatti, S. Prassede, Rome.
1600	*Investiture of St. Hyacinth, Canonization of St. Hyacinth by Pope Clement VIII,* and *The World of Christians,* (vault) Cappella Ascoli, S. Sabina, Rome (cat.nos. 99, 100).
1604	*Madonna and Child with Zuccaro family as Donors* for S. Caterina, S. Angelo in Vado. *Emissary of St. Charles to Cardinal Borromeo,* Collegio Borromeo, Pavia, for Federico Borromeo. Hall of the Zodiac, Palazzo Marozzi, Pavia (cat. no. 104)
	At Arona on Lago Maggiore. *Pietà with Saints Bernard and Mary* and *Dead Christ with Angels* for a chapel on one of the Borromeo

Islands (cf. cat. no. 101).

1605	*Lettere e Principi et Signori Amatori del Disegno, Pittura, Scultura et Architettura* and *Lament of Painting* published in Mantua.
1605-07	At Savoy court in Turin. Frescoes for gallery (lost) connecting Palazzo Madama with new Palace of Carl Emmanuel I.
1607	*Idea dei Pittori, Scultori et architetti* published.
1608	*Dimora in Parma* and *Passagio per l'Italia* published in Bologna. *Disrobing of Christ* for S. Rocco, Parma. *Vision of St. Catherine of Vigri.*
1609	Dies in Ancona, August 6.

CATALOGUE

Dimensions

Measurements of drawings are given in millimeters and inches, height preceding width.

Medium

Unless otherwise specified the term *ink* refers to brown ink. Paper is specified only in cases where the sheet is tinted.

References

Unless cited in full, exhibition and bibliographical references are indicated by a short form consisting of the location or author's name and date of publication. Complete citations are listed under the short form in the bibliography.

Exhibitions without a catalogue are not normally cited.

TADDEO ZUCCARO

1 *Five Walking Figures* early 1550's
verso: *Back of Male Nude with Raised Arm and other Studies*

Pen and ink with brown wash over black chalk, heightened with white.
Verso: red chalk
244 x 215 mm. (9 ⁹⁄₁₆ x 8 ⅜ inches)
Duke Roberto Ferretti, Montreal

PROVENANCE: Sale, Christie's London, 8 December 1987, lot 74.

LITERATURE: unpublished

EXHIBITIONS: none

John Gere correctly identified this drawing as an early work by Taddeo and originally thought it might possibly be a study of apostles for an *Assumption of the Virgin*. Later, he suggested that it might come from a scene of Roman history (correspondence from the owner 16 October 1988). Certainly either suggestion is plausible, although in a scene from Roman history one expects the presence of leggings on the figures, unless a group of philosophers or statesmen is intended. The frieze-like arrangement of the figures is quite typical of Taddeo's manner of composition during his early years while still within the sphere of Polidoro's influence.

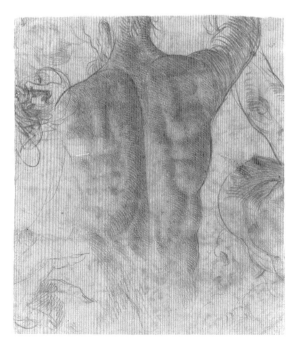

1 *verso*

1 *recto*

The stylistic compatibility between this drawing and the *Shepherds Dancing Round a Bonfire* in Budapest (Gere 1969a, pl.6), particularly the broad, planar description of the legs and equally broad application of wash, is evident as Gere suggests.

The resolution of the styles of drawing found in this sheet and other assumed early works in this exhibition and elsewhere present obstacles to the viewer as he attempts to arrive at a fuller understanding of Taddeo's early style. If this very early group of drawings, all without a link to a documented surviving commission, is actually from Taddeo's hand, the viewer is faced with the task of explaining, or at least accepting, a tremendous acceleration in quality within his *oeuvre* during the decade of the 1550's. While not without precedent, this rapid development requires something of a leap of faith on the student's part. In no way does a presumed early drawing such as this actually prepare one for the sophistication of the drawings for the Mattei or Frangipani chapels, some datable to the mid-1550's.

TADDEO ZUCCARO

2   *Four Standing Figures* c. 1550

Pen and ink with brown wash over traces of black chalk
204 x 124 mm. (8 x 4 ⅞ inches)
Private Collection

PROVENANCE: H.M. Calmann(?), London; P.& D. Colnaghi, London.

LITERATURE: Gere 1969a, p.215, no.251, pl.20.

EXHIBITIONS: none

This drawing, in its use of wash, arrangement of figures in a manner suggesting a Roman frieze, and antique costumes, suggests an early drawing by Taddeo, possibly in connection with a façade decoration in the manner of Polidoro da Caravaggio. The handling of pen and wash comes closest to that in the copy of part of an antique relief of *The Fall of Phaeton* in the British Museum (1859-8-6-78, Gere 1969a, pl.18) and that in Duke Ferretti's collection (cat. no. 1).

2

ATTRIBUTED TO TADDEO ZUCCARO

3   *Studies for Two Recumbent Allegorical Figures Seen from Below* c. 1550

Inscribed on mount in the hand of the owner of the "Borghese Album":*S.B. no.69*. Extensive inventory annotation on verso with *S.B. no.25* in Resta's (?) hand.
Pen and ink with brown wash over black chalk
157 x 220 mm. (6 ⅛ x 8 ⅝ inches)
Yale University Art Gallery, New Haven, Everett V. Meeks, B.A. 1901 Fund, 1986.92.1

PROVENANCE: Sebastiano Resta(?); Sagredo Collection, Venice (?); Prince Borghese, Rome (the so-called Borghese Albums); sold Lyon ca. 1910; Maurice Marignane, Paris by descent to his son Hubert de Marignane; sold Sotheby's London, 30 June 1986, lot. 174; Mia N. Weiner, New York.

LITERATURE: *The Burlington Magazine,* October, 1986, p.xxvi, repr.

EXHIBITIONS: *Fall Exhibition,* Mia Weiner, New York, 1986.

Listed in the Borghese Album as "Scuola Bolognese" the attribution to Taddeo was made by John Gere and thought to date to around 1550. As an early work of Taddeo, the drawing makes sense as an idea for a façade decoration at a time when the artist was strongly influenced by the exterior decorations of Polidoro (cf. cat. nos. 1,2 and 6) and engaged in a number of decorative projects of his own around Rome, according to Vasari. The extensive use of wash in the drawing is typical of this period with respect to other designs for façades such as the *Studies of a Nude Man with a Cutlass* (Uffizi 11216F Gere 1969a, p. 153, no. 72, pl. 15) and a sheet of figure studies in the National Gallery of Scotland (no. D 3130, see Andrews 1968, no. 891).

The distinctive hinges and the inscription *S.B. no. 25* on the verso of this drawing (as well as the *S.B. no. 69* on the mount are, according to Marignane (see Monte Carlo 1966, pp. 11ff.), characteristic of certain drawings collected by the Milanese cleric Padre Sebastiano Resta (1635-1714). These were the drawings *not* included in the sixteen albums into which Resta pasted the sheets he acquired for his fellow collector the Bishop of Arezzo and which were then acquired by Lord Somers in 1701. All but one of those albums are believed to have been destroyed by fire in 1752. The survivor is the *Galleria Portatile* album now in the Ambrosiana, Milan.

S. B. n° 69.

3

TADDEO ZUCCARO?

4 *Mystic Marriage of Saint Catherine*

Inscribed recto, lower right: 57; verso, lower left: *Ecole de
Parma/Parmegiano.*
Pen and ink with brown wash heightened with white
176 x 116 mm. (7 x 4 ½ inches)
The Art Museum, Princeton University, Gift of Frank Jewett Mather, Jr. 47-
15

PROVENANCE: Thomas Dimsdale, London (Lugt 2426); Paignon
Dijonval; Charles Fairfax Murray; Frank Jewett Mather, Jr. (Lugt supp.
1853a).

LITERATURE: Gibbons 1977, no.705.

EXHIBITION: New York 1930, no.62, as Parmigianino.

This drawing was initially attributed to Parmigianino and later thought a very early work by Taddeo Zuccaro by Gere, who has since had second thoughts about its authorship (correspondence of 30 March 1989). There are certain awkward and overly stiff passages in the drawing, especially where the wash and white heightening have been applied. The pen work, although in parts broken, is more suggestive of Taddeo's hand. These aspects must be considered part of the overall problem of identifying the very earliest drawings by the artist, assuming that the occasional less than fluid sketch is possible during this period.

Although not comparable in overall quality, points of relationship should be sought in such drawings as the *Scene from Roman History* in a private collection (cat. no. 6).

4

TADDEO ZUCCARO

5   *Standing Nude Man* c. 1550
verso: *Three Studies of Soldiers*

Inscribed on verso: *Maturino,* and in graphite in 19th or early 20th century
hand: *P... au Vatican/......Maturino par/Mariette le pere/ Collection van Zande*
Red chalk heightened with white. Verso: red chalk
Watermark: six-pointed star in a circle (not in Briquet)
420 x 287 mm. (16 ½ x 11 ¼ inches)
Metropolitan Museum of Art, New York, Rogers Fund, 68.113

PROVENANCE: F. van de Zande, Paris (Lugt supp.2680); sale, Paris, F.
Guichardot, 30 April 1855; Carl Konig (Lugt 583); sale, Sotheby's London,
11 March 1964, lot 141, as Maturino; Philip Pouncey, London.

LITERATURE: Gere 1969a, p. 179, no. 143, pl. 12 and 14; Bean 1969, p. 312;
Gere 1971, fig. 14; Metropolitan Museum of Art, *Notable Acquisitions,* 1975,
p. 57; Bean 1982, no. 279.

John Gere has identified the superb figure study on the *recto* as a study for the
Roman soldier holding the reins of the horse in the center of the more fully
worked sheet in pen and wash with white heightening in a private collection
(cat. no. 6). The purpose of these drawings as preparatory sketches for a
façade decoration is evident by the planar poses on both sides, suggestive of
Roman reliefs, the form such decorations were supposed to mimic in fresco.

Houses decorated with largely sequential scenes from Roman history were in
fashion in Rome at mid-century and the most active of the artists specializing in
this now lost art form was Polidoro da Caravaggio and his assistant who Vasari
tells us was one Maturino da Firenze (Vasari 1850 III, p. 290ff.). One of the scenes
portrayed by Federico in his life of Taddeo shows the artist copying a Polidoro
façade.

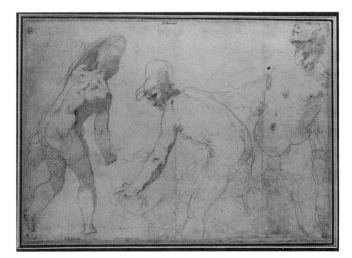

5 verso

5 *recto*

Taddeo himself was actively engaged in such Polidoresque projects beginning in 1548 when he decorated the façade of the Palazzo of Jacopo Mattei with nine scenes from the story of Furius Camillus, now lost. Other façade projects, including scenes from the life of Alexander the Great and the myths involving Mercury were executed around 1550.

The relationship between this sheet of figures and the more highly worked compositional studies such as cat. no. 6 demonstrate an important aspect of Taddeo's working method that recurs throughout his career where individual figure studies are kept on file and integrated into single scenes. The drawing, while probably based on a model, is also indicative of Taddeo's response to Antiquity, reflecting the manner and pose of the sculptural group of the *Dioscuri* on the Capitoline.

TADDEO ZUCCARO

6   *Scene from Roman History* c. 1550

Pen and ink with brown wash and white heightening over traces of black chalk on blue paper
257 x 280 mm. (10 ¼ x 11 ¹/₁₆ inches)
Private Collection

PROVENANCE: William Young Ottley(?);Sir Thomas Lawrence (Lugt 2445, no.26 in Woodburn Gallery sale of Lawrence drawings, 7th exhibition, April, 1836 as Polidoro); Sale, Sotheby's London, 12 March 1963, lot 22 as Federico Zuccaro.

LITERATURE: *Apollo*, February 1963, p.xlvii; Gere 1969a, pp. 38-39 and 214-15, no. 250, pl. 9; Gere 1971, p. 83, pl. XVI.

One of the most accomplished of Taddeo's early drawings, this bold work (like cat. nos. 1-3) stems from Taddeo's intense study of the work of Polidoro in preparation for his own commissions to decorate Roman façades. This is proved by the subject, Roman soldiers in triumph, undoubtedly meant to be read in sequence with other scenes in a frieze-like manner, and the low point of view suggesting a beholder at street level.

While the flamboyant pen work of Taddeo is much in evidence, the wash and heavy application of white heightening lend substance to the drawing. This emphasizes the antique sculptural prototypes that these paintings were meant to copy.

As noted in the preceding entry, the Metropolitan Museum's nude figure served as a model for the soldier holding the reins of the horse in this sketch.

6

TADDEO ZUCCARO

7 *Alexander the Great and Bucephalus* c. 1550

Pen and ink with brown wash
178 x 227 mm. (7 x 8 ⅞ inches)
Woodner Family Collection, New York

PROVENANCE: Sale, Christie's London, 5 July 1983, no.62.

LITERATURE: none

EXHIBITIONS: Cambridge 1985, no.79; London (R.A. Woodner) 1987, no.24.

This drawing, unquestionably by Taddeo, demonstrates the robust use of line and *brio* of execution one looks for in the best of the artist's early drawings. It shows Alexander about to mount his beloved charger Bucephalus. When the animal died in battle, Alexander founded a town, Bucephala, dedicated to the horse and located near the river Hydaspes where the battle was fought.

Taddeo is known to have decorated three buildings with scenes from the life of Alexander: the exterior of a house beside S. Lucia della Tinta (not on the church as noted by Nicholas Turner, London [R.A. Woodner] 1987, no.24) around 1550, and rooms in the Palazzo Caetani in Rome and the Castello Odescalchi at Bracciano. The Woodner drawing bears little resemblance to the surviving drawings for the Palazzo Caetani or the single surviving sketch for the commission at Bracciano. It is, however, stylistically very similar to a drawing at Christ Church, Oxford (Gere 1969a, pl.41) also illustrating *Alexander and Bucephalus* although in a different context with Alexander on his throne, surrounded by male and female figures, the bridled horse held to one side. As Turner correctly notes, the two drawings must certainly date from the same years and it seems likely to suppose they were both meant for the series of six scenes for the anonymous building next to S. Lucia della Tinta.

An iconographical reference to the founding of Bucephala is found in the presence of the river god, reclining to the left, who must refer to the Hydaspes. He seems to hold in his left hand a shovel. The role played by the semi-nude female figure behind the river god is more obscure. The subject manner and the execution of the scene are indicative of Taddeo's work on façade decorations in the manner of Polidoro da Caravaggio during the first few years after the half-century.

TADDEO ZUCCARO

8 *Joseph and Potiphar's Wife*

Pen and ink with brown wash heightened with white on blue prepared paper
132 x 111 mm. (5 ¼ x 4 inches)
Inscribed lower right: 150
Private Collection

PROVENANCE: Jan Pietersz. Zoomer (Lugt 1511); Sir Thomas Lawrence (L.2445); John Viscount Hampden sale, 1827; Mr. and Mrs. Hugh Squire, London; Sale, Sotheby's London, 28 June 1979, lot 32.

LITERATURE: Popham 1953, p. 46 (as source for Parmigianino by Domenico Tibaldi); Gere 1969a, n. 120, pp. 50-51, pl. 34; Popham 1971, pp. 30-31, 270; Ragghianti 1974, pp. 122-123.

EXHIBITIONS: London 1836, no. 10 (as Parmigianino in cartouche by Vasari); London Royal Academy 1960, no. 477 (as Parmigianino); Moir 1986, no. 51.

This drawing was long attributed to Parmigianino owing to the inscription on a seventeenth-century etching after the drawing by Lucas Vorsterman and Hendrik van der Borcht and an inscription in an eighteenth-century hand on the original mount with its elaborate cartouche (now on deposit at the Fogg Museum and itself wrongly thought to be executed by Vasari). *Joseph and Potiphar's Wife* was first attributed to Taddeo by John Gere and thought to be stylistically in keeping with the artist's early years in Rome. It is, together with a similar drawing in Mr. Gere's own collection, a preparatory sketch for an etching by Bartolomeo Passarotti (Bartsch xviii, p. 2, no. 1), made around 1550, at a time when the two artists were sharing quarters. The etching measures 164 x 130 mm., roughly the same size as the two drawings. It is logically assumed that the more quickly sketched work in the Gere collection preceded the present, more fully worked drawing. Both, however, capture the urgency of the moment, an aspect lost to a considerable degree in the etching.

The subject is assumed to be the moment from Genesis 39: 6-20 where Joseph attempts to escape the advances of the wife of the Pharaoh. This is more apparent in the London drawing for it is the only one of the four versions where the activity clearly takes place in an interior.

8

TADDEO ZUCCARO

9 *Two Flying Putti and an Urn* c. 1555

Black and white chalk on blue paper
241 x 383 mm. (9 ½ x 15 inches)
Cooper-Hewitt Museum, The Smithsonian Institution's National Museum
of Design, New York, Friends of the Museum Fund 1901-39-108

PROVENANCE: Giovanni Piancastelli.

LITERATURE: Gere 1969a, p. 178, no. 139, pl. 80.

Originally attributed to Annibale Carracci by Philip Pouncey, this drawing was given to Taddeo Zuccaro by John Gere and thought to have served as a sheet of studies for spandrel figures. A natural comparison is suggested by the artist's similar studies in Amsterdam and Leiden for the decoration of the Frangipani Chapel (Gere 1969a, nos. 1 and 89). A potential use, directly or indirectly through Federico, for a commission such as the Casino of Pius IV of 1561-63, where an abundance of such *putti* are found cannot be ruled out.

STUDIES FOR THE MATTEI CHAPEL, S. MARIA DELLA CONSOLAZIONE 10-12

TADDEO ZUCCARO

10   *The Agony in the Garden*
verso: *Study of a Leg*

Pen and ink and wash over black chalk. Verso: red chalk. Watermark: Sea
horse with a vessel
225 x 192 mm. (8 ⅞ x 7 ½ inches) irregularly cut at top
Art Gallery of Ontario, Gift of Marvin Gelber 87/140

PROVENANCE: H.M. Calmann; Sale, Sotheby's London, 4 July 1975, lot 86.

LITERATURE: Gere 1963, p. 393, fig. 9; Gere 1969a, cat. no. 117, pp. 66, 170, 217.

EXHIBITION: McTavish 1981-82, no. 29.

Included under the heading of the Mattei Chapel decorations, this drawing
has a complex inter-relationship with that commission. Taddeo depicted *The
Agony in the Garden* three times, once on the vault of the Mattei Chapel, a
second time in the panel painting now preserved in Zagreb (see Gere 1963) and
third in a composition from the life of Christ possibly engraved by Cornelis Cort
(see Zeri 1957, fig. 37). The entire vault was engraved in 1615 by Jacob Matham.
As Gere has rightly pointed out, the Toronto sketch can be attributed to Taddeo
and is closest to the Zagreb painting, although it is probably a first idea and
several changes were incorporated into the finished composition. The apostle on
the left is most literally maintained in the final picture and is the thread that
connects several other drawings of the subject by different hands (one in the
Albertina given to Trometta, a second attributed to Barocci in the Teyler
Museum, Haarlem and a third given to an unknown follower of Taddeo but
strongly resembling Trometta as well, from the Earl of Plymouth's collection
sold at Christie's, 1 July 1986, lot 113). Gere suggests that this easel painting was
the one offered to Niccolo Gaddi, a Florentine collector in 1579.

The other two foreground figures, particularly the one in the center with the
very limply hanging right arm, come closer to the figural elements of the Mattei
Chapel. They are worked out further by Taddeo in a drawing at Windsor (Gere
1969a, fig. 68).

A copy after the composition is in the Kupferstichkabinett in East Berlin
(20201).

10

Several applications of the same motives for different purposes developed by Taddeo during the years 1553-1558 were the standard procedure rather than the exception. That he should manage this kind of reinterpretation between fresco and oil painting is a reaffirmation of the artist's inventiveness and mutability.

11 *Study of a Man Seen from Behind* c. 1555

Red chalk heightened with white.
344 x 188 mm. (13 ⁹/₁₆ x 7 ³/₁₆ inches)
National Gallery of Art, Washington, D.C., Ailsa Mellon Bruce Fund
1972.4.2.

PROVENANCE: A.P.E. Gasc (Lugt 1131); Yvonne Tan Bunzl (her catalogue, 23 Nov. - 8 Dec.1971, no. 55).

LITERATURE: Washington 1974a, no. 17; Washington 1978, p. 46.

EXHIBITIONS: none

Few individual figure studies survive for the Mattei Chapel, S. Maria della Consolazione, Rome. This very dynamically drawn figure has been thought to be a preliminary study for the servant climbing the stairs in Taddeo's fresco of *The Last Supper* (fig. 1). The entire composition was engraved by Aliprando Caprioli in 1575 and Jacob Matham in 1616.

While it is true that the upper torso of the figure corresponds to the fresco, the legs are quite differently arranged. The National Gallery figure was studied as a running, not climbing figure, and it is likely that it served a dual purpose, that in *The Last Supper* but also as a study for a figure later omitted from *The Betrayal of Christ* in the same chapel. Comparison with a drawing in the Bode Museum, East Berlin (120-1989, a sheet from the Vasari *Libro* of several figural groups for this fresco) yields an important comparison (fig. 2). On the right side of the central group in the middleground is another use for the National Gallery figure, as a soldier running to arrest Christ. As demonstrated in his work on the Frangipani Chapel, Taddeo would often work out solutions to two or more

fig. 1, Taddeo Zuccaro, *The Last Supper*, Mattei Chapel, S. Maria della Consolazione, Rome

fig. 2, Taddeo Zuccaro, *Arrest of Christ*, Staatliche Museen zu Berlin, East Berlin

11

compositions at once, thus his double application of the Washington D.C. figure comes as no surprise.

This drawing is further evidence of the tremendous influence Michelangelo's Pauline Chapel frescoes had on Taddeo's art. It fits firmly into the *milieu* of the *Conversion of Paul* by Michelangelo with its abundance of repoussoir figures.

TADDEO ZUCCARO

12 *A Soldier Running* c. 1553

Pen and ink with brown wash, heightened with white on faded blue paper
369 x 215 mm. (14 ½ x 8 ½ inches)
Cooper-Hewitt Museum, The Smithsonian Institution's National Museum
of Design, New York 1938.88.4496

PROVENANCE: unknown

LITERATURE: Gere 1963, p. 391, n. 5; Gere 1969a, p. 178, no. 140.

EXHIBITIONS: none

John Gere was the first to identify this drawing as a study for the soldier running in the left foreground of *The Betrayal of Christ* in the Mattei Chapel (fig. 3). Its problematic condition interferes somewhat with its quality which falls considerably short of the red chalk study for the same commission in Washington (cat. no. 11).

fig. 3, Taddeo Zuccaro, *Arrest of Christ*, Mattei Chapel, S. Maria della Consolazione, Rome

12

There are drawings related to this one in Berlin (Bode Museum, 120-1989) and Paris (Louvre 6745), of which a copy exists at Christ Church, Oxford. The Cooper-Hewitt drawing has most in common in regard to size, style and technique with the Louvre sheet. Also of related interest is another drawing in the Cooper-Hewitt collection (1931-66-40), unconvincingly attributed to Federico of *Three Disciples*, copied after the group in the lower left of *Christ Washing the Disciples Feet* in the vault of the Mattei Chapel adjacent to the *Betrayal*.

TADDEO ZUCCARO

13 *Figure of a Youth*
verso: *Figure of a Man*

Pen and black and brown ink with gray wash and traces of white heightening over red chalk.
266 x 176 mm. (10 ½ x 6 ⅞ inches)
Fogg Art Museum, Harvard University, Cambridge, Massachusetts
Bequest of Charles A. Loeser 1932.299

PROVENANCE: Paul Sandby, London (Lugt 2112).

LITERATURE: Mongan-Sachs 1940, no. 246; Oberhuber 1979, no. 24.

EXHIBITIONS: Tokyo 1979, no. 22.

Formerly given to Correggio, then to Cigoli, this drawing has been attributed to Taddeo by Oberhuber, Röttgen and Kirwin. There is no reason to doubt the present attribution. The lively pen work and elongated treatment of hands suggest that, while the drawing does not seem to relate to a specific figure in a commission, it should be assigned to the period of Taddeo's work on the Mattei Chapel in S. Maria della Consolazione around 1553-56, possibly the latter year based on the puckish physiognomic similarities and horn-like curls of the Harvard youth with the figure in the foreground pouring the wine in the *Last Supper* in the Mattei Chapel (see fig. 1), and the figure who helps support Eutychus in the Metropolitan Museum's study for *St. Paul Restoring Eutychus to Life* from the Frangipani Chapel commission (cat. no. 16).

Certainly the handling of the pen and ink has a great deal in common with the study for one of the Sibyls in the lunette of the Mattei Chapel presently in the collection of Mr. Carter Jonas.

13

TADDEO ZUCCARO

14 *The Healing of a Demoniac Woman* c. 1557

Red chalk, brush and red wash on tan paper.
290 x 220 mm. (11 $^7/_{16}$ x 8 $^{11}/_{16}$ inches)
Cleveland Museum of Art, Gift of Robert Hays Gries, 39.662

PROVENANCE: John Barnard, London (Lugt 1420); Dr. Daniel A.
Heubsch, Cleveland; Dr. Robert Hays Gries, Cleveland.

LITERATURE: Gere and Pouncey 1983, p. 207 under no. 331.

EXHIBITIONS: Olzewski 1981, no.79 (repr.); Notre Dame 1983, p.14, no.48.

Gere (written communication 6 December 1978) has suggested that this drawing is one of several studies possibly intended for an unexecuted altarpiece in the chapel dedicated to San Filippo Benizzi in S. Marcello al Corso. The subject was to have been *San Filippo Benizzi Healing the Possessed Woman*. Benizzi was the founder of the Servite Order whose church in Rome was S. Marcello al Corso, the location of the Frangipani Chapel. A sheet of quick sketches for the same composition is in the Uffizi (10995F, Gere 1966, fig.10) and a more fully worked out compositional idea is in the British Museum (1946-7-13-567, Gere 1969a, pl.105).

A number of connoisseurs, Oberhuber, Olzewski, Gregori, Vitzthum, Alasko, and Fernandez-Gimenez among them, believe that the Cleveland drawing, originally attributed to Domenichino, might be the work of Federico. This notion should be abandoned based on the close parallel with the figures on the right side of the British Museum drawing who attend to the possessed woman and serve as a bracketing device around the saint. The pose of the possessed woman is altered, but maintains the pose of one arm thrust up and the other downwards. The British Museum sketch shows her with her back to the viewer gesturing toward Saint Filippo. All this suggests Taddeo's method of attempting various solutions to important figures in a composition, particularly of visualizing a dramatic gesture from several points of view. He did this previously in the same chapel as he synthesized the pose of St.Paul in the *Blinding of Elymas* and the *Healing of the Cripple* (see cat nos. 15, 17, 18 and 20). Federico tended not to work in this manner. The Cleveland drawing is also fully in keeping with the other sketches for the Frangipani Chapel in its high level of histrionic gesturing, an aspect of late Mannerist compositional bombast one is more apt to see in the earlier work of Taddeo. There is also the question of

14

quality that the drawing exhibits, especially a quality and ease in execution that Federico would not have been capable of at this period of his career.

An aspect of the technique employed in the Cleveland drawing also supports an attribution to Taddeo. Here, the artist uses red washes on the figures, as in the drawing at the Art Institute of Chicago (cat. no. 15), a drawing that is stylistically close in the use of the wide parallel hatching along the face and drapery of both figures. Thus, the dating should be placed at around 1557 for both drawings.

Olzewski has noted that the pose of the demoniac woman is based on the possessed youth in Raphael's *Transfiguration*, datable to 1519-20. Inspiration from the Roman works of Michelangelo and Raphael were much more important to Taddeo than to Federico who was influenced more by his brother's ideas than by the preceding generation of masters.

EXHIBITED IN NEW YORK ONLY

STUDIES FOR THE FRANGIPANI CHAPEL, S. MARCELLO AL CORSO 15-21

TADDEO ZUCCARO

15 *Sheet of Studies for the Blinding of Elymas, Sacrifice at Lystra, and a Holy Family* c. 1557 verso: *Three Men Supporting a Fourth*

Inscribed verso upper left: *favi-4*
Pen and ink with brush and brown wash, black and red chalks with red chalk wash. No visible watermark.
386 x 274 mm. (15 ¼ x 10 ¾ inches)
Art Institute of Chicago, Gift of Robert B. Harshe 1928.196

PROVENANCE: Possibly William Young Ottley, London, sale: London T. Philippe, 20 June 1814, lot 1492 (as Taddeo), see Lugt, p.501; Sir Thomas Lawrence (Lugt 2445) sale, London, Christie's 4 June 1860, lot 108 (as Michelangelo); Mr. Annesley Gore, Los Angeles; Robert B. Harshe, Chicago.

LITERATURE: Gere 1969a, pp. 73-74, 76-77, 138, no.22, pls. 94-95, pp. 211-12, under 241; Gere 1971, pp. 17, 83. pl. 17; Joachim and McCullagh 1979, no. 28, pl. 36; Rome 1984, p. 114.

EXHIBITIONS: Vitzthum 1970, no. 10, repr.; Nielson 1972, no. 12 repr.; Feinblatt 1976, no. 113, repr.; Olszewski 1981, no. 82, repr.

15 *recto*

For good reason, this is one of the most famous drawings by Taddeo and, together with the drawings in Baltimore, New Haven, New York, and Princeton University (cat. nos. 16, 17, 18, 19, 20 and 21) one of several drawings in this exhibition preliminary to the artist's decoration of the Frangipani Chapel in the Roman church of San Marcello al Corso with scenes from the life of Saint Paul (fig. 4). It is among the most spirited sheets of studies by the artist, reflecting not only *primo pensieri* for the frescoes but also his effort to capture the shock and surprise of the proconsul of Asia, Sergius Paulus, that will end in his conversion to Christianity (Acts 13:8-12).

On the left hand margin Taddeo has sketched two groups of bystanders with Elymas, arching to the left and reaching for his eyes, the solution ultimately used in the fresco but altered in a drawing at Windsor (Gere 1969a, fig. 88). The second sketch depicts St. Paul, with his back toward the viewer, striding into the group. This approach to the figure was abandoned in the final result but is reiterated in the fully worked figure study in the Albertina (Gere 1969a, fig. 101). The group to the right of the striding St. Paul probably relates to the New Haven drawing, (cat. no. 18). The *recto* of the Chicago drawing also contains what might be, in the opinion of John Gere, a study for a discarded composition for the Frangipani Chapel, the *Sacrifice at Lystra* and a *Holy Family with the Infant St. John the Baptist* in the lower center.

Throughout, in the preparatory studies for the chapel's frescoes, it is of interest how Taddeo digests the achievement of Raphael's tapestry cartoons in similar narratives while simultaneously acknowledging a debt to Michelangelo in the physicality of his subjects. Whereas in Raphael's *modello* for *The Blinding of Elymas*, the center of the composition and the narrative is the conversion of the enthroned proconsul, Taddeo makes the blinding of the Jew itself the dramatic focus in the final painting, a marked departure from his earlier conception of the subject recorded in a drawing at Windsor.

Because both sides of the other drawings related to this commission portray additional motives from the Frangipani Chapel decorations, it is natural that previous writers have suggested that the *verso* of the Chicago drawing is a very early idea for the *Raising of Eutychus*. While this is entirely possible, it might also portray the *Deposition* or *Lamentation of Christ*, particularly when viewed in relationship with a drawing such as that in the Ashmolean given to Michelangelo (fig. 5) a drawing not too distant in its style from Taddeo's own work in chalk from this period. In the right hand margin on the *recto* of the Princeton drawing (cat. no. 17) is also what appears to be a small study for a

fig. 4, Taddeo Zuccaro, *The Blinding of Elymas*, Mattei
Chapel, S. Maria della Consolazione, Rome

fig. 5, Michelangelo, *The Deposition*,
Ashmolean Museum, Oxford

15 *verso*

Lamentation surrounded by a rectangular margin. Taddeo would later return to
the group on the *verso* of the Art Institute's drawing when he began to compose
the *Martyrdom of Saint Lawrence* for S. Lorenzo in Damaso as indicated by the
pose of Saint Lawrence and the figures around him in the sketch also in the
Ashmolean (ill. in Gere 1966a, fig. 2).

The decorations for the Frangipani Chapel were commissioned of Taddeo
between 1556 and 1558. He was still working on the commission at his death in
1566.

TADDEO ZUCCARO

16 *Saint Paul Restoring Eutychus to Life* c. 1557-58

Pen and ink, brown wash heightened with white over black chalk on gray paper
337 x 461 mm. (13 ¼ x 18 ⅛ inches)
Metropolitan Museum of Art, New York, Rogers Fund 67.188

PROVENANCE: Prof. Einar Perman, Stockholm

LITERATURE: Gere 1966, pp. 25-26, see no. 27; Bean 1968, p. 86; Gere 1969a, no. 142, pl. 84; Byam Shaw 1976, I, p. 152, see no. 534; Bean 1982, no. 280; Rome 1984, p. 113.

This large and exquisitely executed drawing is another study for one of the frescoed decorations of the Frangipani Chapel in S. Marcello al Corso. The final look of the fresco is much altered, only the grouping of figures around the fallen Eutychus being retained. As in the *Blinding of Elymas* the slightly repoussoir posture of Saint Paul with its strong *contrapposto* was changed to a figure seen almost frontally, a decision (possibly made by Federico Zuccaro after the artist's death?) resulting in a more prosaic and psychologically less convincing connection to the narrative.

The Metropolitan Museum drawing shares with the few surviving highly worked drawings for this commission a truly Michelangelesque physicality, influenced no doubt by the experience of the Pauline Chapel in the Vatican. This is evidently the source for Taddeo's frequent use of repoussoir figures and, perhaps, even the figure of Eutychus is modeled on Saint Peter in the Florentine's *Crucifixion of Peter* for the chapel. There are also the pronounced claw-like hands common to this drawing and the Lehman Collection *Martyrdom of Saint Paul* (cat. no. 19) and what appears to be a copy after the lost altarpiece in S. Marcello al Corso of the *Conversion of Paul* (Munich, art market). The figure who holds the blinded tax collector in that drawing is clearly a reprise of the same figure in Michelangelo's fresco of the same subject.

An earlier study for this subject is at Christ Church, Oxford and a copy after the entire composition is in the collection of the Fitzwilliam Museum, Cambridge. The sketch on the *verso* of the Art Institute of Chicago's drawing (cat. no. 15) has nothing in common with the Eutychus composition and should not be considered further as relating to the Frangipani Chapel commission.

16

TADDEO ZUCCARO

17 *Kneeling Male Nude, Studies for the Nailing of Christ to the Cross and for the Virgin Fainting at the Foot of the Cross; Two Heads; Architectural Sketches*
verso: *Studies of Heads, Figures and Architecture; Circles Drawn with a Compass*

Pen and ink with brown wash over black chalk. Verso: Pen and ink with some brown wash. Watermark: unidentified, probably a dagger
280 x 297 mm. (11 x 11 ¾ inches)
The Art Museum, Princeton University, Gift of Frank Jewett Mather, Jr.
53-38

PROVENANCE: Frank Jewett Mather, Jr. (Lugt supp.1853a)

LITERATURE: Scholz 1967, p. 294, figs. 28,29; Gere 1969a, pp.73f, 203; Gibbons 1977, p. 218, no. 706.

EXHIBITIONS: none

This drawing fits well into the sequence of quick studies for different aspects of the Frangipani Chapel found in Chicago and New Haven (cat. nos. 15 and 18). The kneeling male nude, a study for the cripple on the left in *The Healing of the Cripple* is the most recognizable connection with the chapel. It was this figure that allowed the firm attribution to Taddeo by Philip Pouncey. John Gere later suggested that the group on the *verso* in the upper right corner was an idea for the group of bystanders at the right of the fresco. This is confirmed by the correspondence noted above (cat. no. 15) with the New Haven

94

17 verso

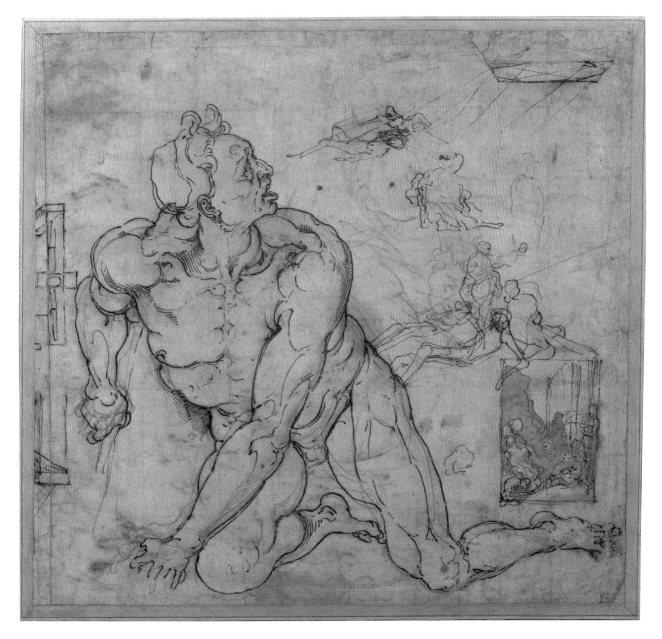

17 *recto*

drawing, which carries two similar groups of figures each featuring, as does the Princeton sketch, the figure with the outstretched arms. The heads on the *verso* might be individual ideas for the features of the bystanders.

The quality of the drawings on the Princeton sheet is also somewhat uneven, several of the female heads being more weakly executed than other studies. Thus, if as Gibbons suggests, the sketches represent several different periods in the artist's career, they also might reflect more than one hand.

Of interest among the three sheets of sketches in Chicago, New Haven and Princeton is that three different types of drawings are shared among them. Each has specific ideas for the frescoes of the Frangipani Chapel. The Princeton and

New Haven drawings have architectural studies and the Chicago and Princeton drawings have separate studies, marked by rectangular framing borders, for subjects from the life of Christ, the Holy Family (Chicago) and Mary swooning at the foot of the cross or, possibly, the Lamentation (Princeton). Gere had suggested that they might be connected with Taddeo's earlier commission for the Mattei Chapel, a possibility worth considering although only one of these subjects, *The Virgin Swooning at the Foot of the Cross*, emerges in the final fresco cycle.

TADDEO ZUCCARO

18 *Studies for the Frangipani Chapel, S.Marcello al Corso* verso: *Studies for the Lunette of the Frangipani Chapel and anArchitectural Design* c. 1558-66

Pen and ink with brown wash over black chalk. Verso: Pen and ink and black chalk.
344 x 270 mm. (13 ⅜ x 10 ¼)
Private Collection, New Haven

PROVENANCE: Giovanni Morelli (Lugt 1902); Dubini Collection (Lugt 987a); Hepley Collection; Armando Neerman.

LITERATURE: none

EXHIBITED: London, National Book League, 1975.

Of all the surviving studies for the Frangipani Chapel this previously unpublished one is most similar to the Art Institute's sketch (cat. no. 15) in its technique and handling of pen and ink. The *recto* probably

18 verso

18 *recto*

represents two abandoned solutions for the group of bystanders to the right of St. Paul in the *Healing of the Cripple*. Only the uppermost figure with his arms outstretched was retained in the final fresco. A very similar study for the same group appears in the upper right of the *verso* of the sheet at Princeton (cat. no. 17), the *recto* of which is dominated by a figure study for the cripple. Another related sketch for this group is in the Uffizi (1099F, ill. in Gere 1969a, pl. 87).

Furthermore, the group of figures on the right side almost seem to complete the similarly sketched figures on the left side of a drawing of *St. Paul* in the Albertina (inv. 625, illustrated in Stix and Fröhlich-Bum 1932, fig. 257) intended as a possible solution for the saint in the *Healing of the Cripple*.

The figures on the *verso* correspond more closely to the angels in the left portion of the lunette above the altarpiece. Other sketches relating to the lunette figures survive in the Seilern Collection of the Courtauld Institute, London and the Leiden University Printroom (see Gere 1969a, figs. 99 a-c). It is likely that the architectural sketch is an idea for the elevation of the altar wall of the chapel.

TADDEO ZUCCARO

19 *The Martyrdom of Saint Paul* c. 1557-58

Inscribed on verso in seventeenth century hand: *Taddeo Zuccaro 5.4*
Pen and ink with brown wash, heightened with white over traces of black chalk
495 x 368 mm. (19 ½ x 14 ⁷⁄₁₆ inches)
Metropolitan Museum, New York, Robert Lehman Collection, 1975.553

PROVENANCE: Sir Peter Lely (Lugt 2092).

LITERATURE: Gere 1969a, p. 180. no. 147, pl. 82; Szabó 1975, pp. 104, 178; Bean 1982, p. 278; Szabó 1983, no. 44; Gere and Pouncey 1983, I, p. 233.

EXHIBITIONS: New York 1965, no. 135; Tokyo 1977, no. 12; New York 1979, no. 38, illus.; Notre Dame 1983, no. 51.

This well known and very important drawing is a study for the fresco in the center of the vault of the Frangipani Chapel and dates with the other drawings for this project to the years 1557-8 (fig. 6). In style, it is most analogous with cat. no. 16, also in the Metropolitan Museum, of *St. Paul*

fig. 6., Taddeo Zuccaro, *The Martyrdom of St. Paul*, Frangipani Chapel, S. Marcello al Corso

19

Restoring Eutychus to Life. It should also be understood to be of stylistic consonance with the two-sided sheet in the Pierpont Morgan Library depicting *The Preaching of St. John the Baptist* and a chalk study on the *verso* that must be a preparatory sketch for the figure of the saint (cat. no. 22).

Several copies of the Lehman drawing are known. They are in the British Museum (5211-50 and 5237-128), the Louvre (11558), the Art Museum, Princeton University (51-114), and the Royal Library, Turin (inv. no. 16047 listed as a copy after Tibaldi).

Lasko in the 1983 Notre Dame exhibition has suggested that the composition was influenced by Parmigianino's *Martyrdom of Saints Peter and Paul* known through Caraglio's engraving.

EXHIBITED IN NEW YORK ONLY

TADDEO ZUCCARO

20 *Standing Male Figure with Arm Raised (St. Paul)*
    verso: *Two Studies of the Same Figure*

Inscribed on verso in old hand: *ro da Sn Agnolo di urbino*
and in a more recent hand: *F. Zuccaro*
Pen and ink with brown wash heightened with white on blue paper,
squared in black chalk. Verso: black chalk
370 x 195 mm. (14 ½ x 7 ¾ inches)
Baltimore Museum of Art, Gift of Saidie A. May, 1928.1.6

PROVENANCE: Saidie A. May, Baltimore.

LITERATURE: Gere 1969a, p. 132, no. 3.

EXHIBITIONS: none

Gere first registered some doubt regarding this drawing in a letter of 25
June 1965 and suggested that it might be the work of Federico copying a
motif of Taddeo's seen in a drawing in Stockholm (Gere 1969a, pl. 100).
He later altered this view and was willing to give the drawing "the benefit of the
doubt," assigning it to Taddeo. In spite of some hardness to the execution the
drawing should rightly be considered to be from Taddeo's hand and associated
with the studies of the prophets for the Frangipani Chapel, particularly with the
drawing in Berlin, which, while executed in a different technique has the same
intensity and interest in sharp, sculptural lighting effects.

That this drawing is a study for St. Paul from the *Healing of the Cripple* is clear,
as Gere rightly points out, from the presence of the curved stairs that appear to
the left of the figure. It has a somewhat complex relationship to some of the
other preparatory sketches for the Frangipani Chapel as well. On the *verso*, in
addition to a large figure of the saint in chalk that reproduces the figure on the

20 verso

20 *recto*

recto, is a quick sketch of the figure with his arm in two positions, brought farther forward and also lowered as found in the fresco. The former stance is identical to that of the saint in the Albertina (inv. 625, Gere 1969a, p. 211-12, no. 241) that Gere connected with the Art Institute's study for the chapel (cat. no.

15). Like the Chicago drawing as well as those at Princeton and in the New Haven private collection (cat. nos. 17 and 18), the Albertina sheet includes smaller quick sketches. Furthermore, the loosely outlined figures on the left border of the Albertina drawing almost appear to complete the figural group on the right side of the New Haven sketch. Therefore, the connections among these studies argue convincingly that the Baltimore drawing be accepted as belonging to this group.

Another version of this drawing, presumably a copy, measuring 447 x 254 mm. in brown ink heightened with white over black chalk was sold at Sotheby's, London 30 March 1987, lot 218.

TADDEO ZUCCARO

21 *Standing Prophet in a Niche Holding a Book*

Pen and ink with brown wash, over black chalk, on brownish paper
404 x 144 mm. (16 x 5 ¾ inches)
Inscribed lower right: *k. 180* and on old mount in Richardson's hand:
Mecarino da Siena
Metropolitan Museum of Art, Gift of Walter Lowry, New York 57.32.2

PROVENANCE: Padre Sebastiano Resta; John, Lord Somers (Lugt 2981); Jonathan Richardson, Sr. (Lugt 2995); Sir Joshua Reynolds (Lugt 2364); William Roscoe, Liverpool; Roscoe sale, Liverpool, Winstanley, 23-28 Sept. 1816, no. 92, as Beccafumi; Walter Lowry, New York.

LITERATURE: Gere 1969a, p. 176 under no. 134 (as a copy); Harprath 1977, pp. 174-175 under no. 124 (as a copy); Bean 1982, no. 281.

EXHIBITIONS: none

This drawing, traditionally ascribed to Beccafumi, was first connected by John Gere with other studies in Munich, Berlin and Angers for the prophets painted on the entrance pilasters of the Frangipani Chapel (fig. 7). His opinion that it is a copy was at first supported by Harprath, who later, after seeing the drawing, accepted it as a work by Taddeo. This opinion has been assumed by Bean. The drawing is admittedly less strong in its characterization than others by Taddeo but its condition may be a factor in this regard. Vasari makes a point of telling us that Taddeo employed numerous assistants on the Frangipani Chapel commission and one must assume that a certain number of his drawings for the commission were copied by assistants.

fig. 7, Taddeo Zuccaro, *Prophet*, Frangipani
Chapel, S. Marcello al Corso, Rome

21

TADDEO ZUCCARO

22 *The Baptist Preaching in the Wilderness* c. 1558
verso: *A Kneeling Male Figure*

Inscribed on Vasari mount in a cartouche on recto: *Taddeo Zuchero/ Da S.
Agnolo/ Pittore* and in a cartouche on verso: *Taddeo Zuchero Da S./Agnolo Pit.*
Also on mount in another hand: *A. 12. Ld Bentink Col* and *Wellesly Coll.*
Pen and ink with brown wash, heightened with white on blue paper
Verso: black and white chalk on blue paper. Watermark: two arrows
crossed (cf. Briquet 6299).
337 x 235 mm. (13 ¼ x 9 ¼ inches)
The Pierpont Morgan Library, New York, The Janos Scholz Collection
1973.26

PROVENANCE: Giorgio Vasari; Bentinck (?); Horace Walpole (according
to Mr. Scholz's records); Janos Scholz, New York.

LITERATURE: Gere 1969a, p. 181, no. 152, repr. pl.165; Ragghianti 1974, I,
p.147; II, figs. 448, 449; Ryskamp 1984, p.187.

EXHIBITIONS: Indianapolis 1954, no.42, repr.; Stubbe 1963, no.180, fig. 44;
New York 1965; Notre Dame 1970, no. D 25, repr; New York 1971, no.180;
Norton 1971; Oberhuber and Walker 1973, no.6, repr.

Almost more celebrated for its provenance than for its subject matter and execution, this two-sided drawing has much in common with Taddeo's studies for the Frangipani Chapel (cat. nos. 15-21) and should, therefore be dated as early as 1558. The pen work found in *The Baptist Preaching* is practically identical to that in the study for the group of bystanders in the sheet in the New Haven private collection (cat. no. 18). The chalk study of the kneeling man on the *verso* is unquestionably a study for the figure of St. Paul in the scene of his martyrdom on the vaulted ceiling of the chapel. As can be seen in the finished drawing for the entire composition in the Lehman Collection (cat. no. 19) the position of the hands clasped in prayer is used in both drawings although in the finished fresco the saint's hands are crossed under his beard. The

22 verso

22 *recto*

manner of using the chalk is also quite similar to the sheet of studies for the Mattei Chapel recently sold from the Gaud Collection and now on the London art market (Kate Ganz, Ltd., *Master Drawings 1500-1900*, 28th June - 8th July 1989). The style of the drawing on the *recto* is also reminiscent of the studies of Diana and her nymphs in the Metropolitan Museum (cat. nos. 27 and 28). There is no surviving record of a painting by Taddeo of *The Baptist Preaching* and the rare occurrence of the saint in the work of either brother is found only in the decorations at Caprarola (see cat. no. 40).

Much has been made of the drawing's elaborate and illustrious mounting, almost certainly comprising a page from Vasari's *Libro dei disegni*. Although trimmed slightly, the drawing is typical of Vasari's choices for his *Libro*, since it is drawn on both sides and demonstrates a variety of materials and quite different techniques. One disconcerting detail is that the artist's name and town are spelled differently on the Morgan Library mount and on another page from the *Libro* presently in the Bode Museum in East Berlin (cat. no. 11, fig. 2). As can be determined by reading Vasari's life of Taddeo, he held his draftsmanship in the very highest esteem.

TADDEO ZUCCARO

23 *Temperance* c. 1556-62

Inscribed on recto lower left: *Barocj*, on verso top edge: *286* on lower edge: *A 21990(10-27)*
Pen and ink with brown wash, heightened with white, on blue paper
226 x 101 (8 ⅞ x 4 inches)
National Gallery of Canada, Ottawa 6896

PROVENANCE: Unidentified collector's mark; purchased from P. & D. Colnaghi, London, 1957.

LITERATURE: Popham and Fenwick 1965, no. 40; Gere 1969a, p. 182, no. 153; Smith 1970; Smith 1973, p. 88, fig. 8; Smith 1977, pp. 65-66; Smith 1978b, p. 333; Emiliani 1985, vol. 1, p. 23.

EXHIBITIONS: Pillsbury and Richards 1978, no. 7; Washington, D.C. 1988, no. 5.

Possibly the most controversial drawing in the exhibition in terms of its attribution, *Temperance* and its critical history have recently been summarized by David McTavish for the exhibition of drawings from Ottawa shown in that city, Vancouver and Washington (Washington, D.C. 1988, no. 5). Early opinions forwarded by Popham, Gere and Smith at first favored an attribution to Taddeo but both Gere and Smith would later change their minds. Later writers, particularly Pillsbury and McTavish defend an attribution to Barocci.

Smith has made a convincing case that this drawing is a study, with considerable changes, for the painted figure of the Virtue in the coved ceiling of one of the upper rooms of the Casino of Pius IV in the Vatican. While Taddeo is not actually listed as one of the participants in the decorations, it is rightly assumed that he provided his brother Federico with designs for his portions of

23

the commission. As cited below, the Ottawa *Temperance* and Notre Dame *Angel Seated on a Cloud* should be considered together as related to the same moment in Taddeo Zuccaro's career and not Barocci's. Many similar *putti* can be found in the frescoes.

Popham's view that this drawing is by Taddeo when his and Federico's styles were close to one another at the time of the work on the Casino of Pius IV should be accepted, although with the Ottawa drawing appearing more Barocci-like. The compelling link with the much more characteristic hand of Taddeo in the Notre Dame sketch should weigh more heavily on the scales than general similarities pointed to by Pillsbury between the fresco of *Temperance* and painted figures by Barocci. Also not to be discounted is Taddeo's manner of working with greater amounts of white heightening in his drawings during the period of activity in the Mattei Chapel around 1553-56, and in some of the few drawings that survive for the designs he provided Federico for the *Flight into Egypt* and *Nativity* in the Church of S. Maria dell' Orto, Rome in 1558-59 (see Gere 1969a, pp. 97ff). It is reasonable to assume that he continued working in this manner during the period when Federico was engaged to decorate portions of the Casino.

An old copy of *Temperance* is in the collection at Windsor (1396).

TADDEO ZUCCARO

24 *An Angel Seated on a Cloud* c. 1556-1562

Inscribed lower right: *cher. Albert*
Pen and brown and black inks with brown wash heightened with white over traces of black chalk on blue paper
175 x 121 mm. (6 ⅞ x 4 ¾ inches) includes two strips of paper about 10 mm. added on either side.
Notre Dame, The Snite Museum, University of Notre Dame, on extended loan as a promised gift from Mr. John D. Reilly, L.85.45.29

PROVENANCE: Nathaniel Hone, London (Lugt 2793); Roderic Thesiger, London; John Minor Wisdom, Jr., New Orleans.

LITERATURE: Gere 1969a, p. 173, no. 124*

EXHIBITIONS: *Princeton Alumni Collections: Works on Paper*, The Art Museum, Princeton University, 1981, p. 41; Weiner 1985, repr.; Spiro and Coleman 1987, no. 25.

This small, yet very fluid study of a typically Taddean puckish angel was first attributed to the artist by James Byam Shaw. Gere later confirmed the attribution.

The Notre Dame drawing of *An Angel Seated on a Cloud* should be understood in connection with the allegorical figure of *Temperance* in Ottawa (cat. no. 23), a drawing that has sparked considerable difference of opinion with most critics divided between an attribution to Federico Barocci and Taddeo (see McTavish in Washington, 1988, pp. 29-30). Most agree, however that the Ottawa sketch is related to the fresco of the same subject in the Casino of Pius IV in the Vatican of 1561-63.

Both drawings share common materials, techniques and stylistic aspects,

24

although it should be pointed out that the angel demonstrates a greater economy and clarity in the use of the wash and white heightening. Numerous angels in similar poses occur on the walls and ceiling decorations of the Casino, attributed to Barocci and the other artists involved with the decorations (cf. Emiliani 1975, figs. 4-6 and Smith 1977, figs. 54-57). The Ottawa sheet does not suggest the drawing style of Barocci at that moment of his career, as comparison with several sketches for the commission amply demonstrates (Emiliani 1975, figs. 11-14 and 16). Conversely, it should be noted that there are few sheets analogous to the Notre Dame drawing in Taddeo's *oeuvre*, but those that come closest date from the period of the decorations of the Mattei Chapel around 1553-1556 (Gere 1969a, pls. 58, 60, 62 and 64).

ATTRIBUTED TO TADDEO ZUCCARO

25 *Studies of Soldiers*
verso: *St.George and the Dragon*

Pen and ink
133 x 100 mm. (5 ¼ x 3 ⅞ inches)
Fogg Art Museum, Harvard University, Cambridge, Massachusetts Gift of
Mrs. Henry Lyman 1978.87

PROVENANCE: Mrs. Henry Lyman.

LITERATURE: none

EXHIBITIONS: none

The small sketch on the drawing's *recto*, depicting ancient soldiers, a common subject in sixteenth-century Roman art, bears enough stylistic relationship to the work of Taddeo to be tentatively ascribed to him. The subject could almost be a first thought for the soldiers in cat. no. 5, and one is struck by the stylistic similarities when the legs of the figures in the Harvard drawing are compared with their counterparts in no. 5, particularly those sketched in and seen from the rear between the two soldiers in the foreground. A possible relationship with the decoration of the Palazzo Caetani around 1559-60 should not be ruled out altogether (cf. Gere 1969a, pls. 122-129).

The *verso* is perhaps slightly less suggestive of Taddeo's art. It bears no relationship with a known composition by the artist, yet is reminiscent of what might be termed the flavor of Taddeo's draughtmanship.

25 *verso*

25 *recto*

26 *Women Approaching a Small Image of a Bull* c. 1560
verso: *Figure Studies*

Pen and ink with brown wash heightened with white. Verso: pen and ink
and black chalk.
268 x 388 mm. (10 ½ x 15 ¼ inches)
The Pierpont Morgan Library, New York, The Janos Scholz Collection
1973.25.

PROVENANCE: Edme Durand, Paris (Lugt supp.841); Janos Scholz, New
York.

LITERATURE: Gere 1969a, p.180, no.148; Ryskamp 1984, p.187.

EXHIBITIONS: Indianapolis 1954, no. 21 (as Naldini); Oberhuber and
Walker 1973, no.5.

This drawing, puzzling in its iconography, depicts a group of seven women walking toward the left in the direction of (or past) a hill on which rests a small (if read as a foreground element) or large cow or bull. A sword is being passed from the hand of one woman to another. On the hillock is a second small sketch for one of the women. In the background are another pair of figures, one perhaps a soldier, standing between two columns. The scene has been called both a moment from the history of Judith of Bethulia and Iphigenia. Neither interpretation has been entirely accepted. Some Bacchanalian rites involved the castration of a *"vitelo"* by women. It could be conjectured that this sketch pertains to such an obscure ritual.

Philip Pouncey was the first to recognize this drawing as a work by Taddeo. Gere later dated it to around the year 1560. The subject matter and arrangement in a frieze-like manner suggest a rather early drawing by Taddeo when he was actively engaged with façade decorations. The long, rather light pen strokes suggest, alternatively, a moment of stylistic transition. The high-waisted, full hipped and slightly pneumatic quality of the women's forms are late Mannerist elements at their most pronounced in Taddeo's work around the time of the execution of the Mattei Chapel commission.

TADDEO ZUCCARO

27 *Studies for a Circular Composition of Diana and her Nymphs Bathing* c. 1560
verso: *Studies for the same composition*

Inscribed upper center: *Ecole Italienne 16e siècle*
Pen and ink with brown wash
273 x 207 mm. (10 ¾ x 8 ⅛ inches)
Metropolitan Museum of Art, New York, Gift of Walter Lowry, 59.219.3

PROVENANCE: Walter Lowry, New York.

LITERATURE: Gere 1969a, p. 178, no. 141, pl. 121; Gere 1969b, p. 41; Gere
1970, p. 125; Bean 1982, no. 282.

EXHIBITION: New York 1965, no. 134.

Jacob Bean first identified this double-sided sketch as the work of Taddeo, an
attribution adopted by Gere and unchallenged since. The possible function
of this work as a decorative design for maiolica has been discussed by Gere
(1970). The dating is largely a result of this assumption. The following
drawing in this catalogue, also in the Metropolitan Museum's collection, is a
study for the group of nymphs in the right hand portion of the central
composition, apparently a group Taddeo found of particular interest, sketching
it twice more on the *verso*.

In the Louvre (9030) is a full scale *modello* for the composition by Orazio
Sammachini. Gere logically assumes that it was produced some time after 1563
when the two artists were engaged in decorating the Sala Regia in the Vatican.
Gere (1969a, p. 199, no. 205) also attributes a sheet of red chalk studies of a
woman drying herself to Taddeo, although these could conceivably be related to

27 verso

27 *recto*

the figure of Susannah in the painting of *Susannah and the Elders* by Tintoretto in the Kunsthistorisches Museum, Vienna.

Here, Taddeo exclusively uses figures to form a series of braid-like diagonals within and surrounding the composition. His predisposition to Michelangelo could be the source of his thinking in such physical terms, quite unlike Federico who did not understand how the human figure could actually anchor and maintain a compositional idea.

It is compelling to believe that this drawing was the one in the William Young Ottley collection catalogue at the Lawrence Gallery in 1836 as "no.24, The Bath of Diana, an elegant sheet of studies, pen lightly washed with bistre. 11 x 9 ¼ in. From the collection of W.Y. Ottley, Esq." It is further mentioned in the Ottley catalogue as "sketches of Venus bathing *on both sides*." Although the sizes listed vary somewhat and there are no collector's marks visible, the evidence for assuming that the description pertains to the Metropolitan Museum's drawing is persuasive.

TADDEO ZUCCARO

28 *Nymphs Bathing* c. 1560
verso: *Study of a Leg*

Inscribed lower right: *Tadeo Zucchari* and on verso: *Tadeo Zucharo*
Pen and ink with brown wash. Verso: red chalk
123 x 123 mm. (4 ⅞ x 4 ⅞ inches)
Metropolitan Museum of Art, New York, Rogers Fund 1970.101.20

PROVENANCE: Unidentified collector's mark; Professor Einar Perman, Stockholm.

LITERATURE: New York 1965, p. 75 under no. 134; Gere 1969a, p. 209, no. 232; Bean 1982, no. 283.

EXHIBITIONS: New York, 1972, no. 59.

A wholly characteristic study for a compositional group by Taddeo that represents a further working out of the bathing nymphs on the right side of the *recto* of the preceding drawing, also in the Metropolitan Museum. Missing from that drawing, however, is the sense of surprise registered on the faces of the two nymphs who crouch behind the reclining nude looking in our direction.

28 *recto*

29 *Sea Battle in the Gulf of Morbihan* c. 1560-62

Reddish brown wash with white heightening over black chalk. Watermark:
a cardinal's hat (Briquet 3395) Siena, 1560; Rome, 1562.
308 x 436 mm. (12 x 17 inches)
Private Collection

PROVENANCE: Baron von Kuhlen; Pietro Scarpa, Venice.

EXHIBITIONS: Oberhuber 1977, no. 35; Moir 1986, no. 52.

Those scholars who have written on this drawing agree to its workshop status. Nevertheless, the *Sea Battle in the Gulf of Morbihan* reflects an important interlude in the career of Taddeo Zuccaro when, as Vasari informs us, he was called upon by Guidobaldo II della Rovere, Duke of Urbino, to make designs for a maiolica service as a gift for Philip II of Spain. The subjects were chosen from the life of Julius Caesar and executed by the Fontana family workshop. This so-called Spanish service was commissioned in 1560 and finished in 1562, dates that are consistent with the watermark, further evidence that this drawing dates to around 1562. Motifs found in the drawing, particularly the activities of the soldiers in the boats as they sever the rigging of the enemy ships, are also present in the fresco of *The Siege of Tunis* in the Sala Regia at the Vatican, begun by Taddeo around 1564 (fig. 9) The complicated relationship among a number of Zuccaro drawings and surviving maiolica is recounted by John Gere (Gere 1963).

fig. 8, *Wine Cooler*, 1574, maiolica,
Wallace Collection, London

Oberhuber, using Gere's study of Taddeo's relationship to maiolica workshops and designs, suggests that this drawing might represent a design for a lost cistern in the Spanish service. Gere, repeating an observation of Popham's, and others have pointed out the similarities between this drawing and a somewhat smaller one at Windsor (no. 5471, illustrated in Gere 1963, fig. 33, measuring 342 mm. in diameter). It is an interesting coincidence that both drawings are circular compositions trimmed at the same point across the top edge of the design. Popham was also the first to suggest a pendant relationship between the Windsor drawing and another naval battle in the British Museum (this information is mistakenly reversed in Moir's catalogue). The latter drawing corresponds with the design inside a maiolica wine cistern in the Bargello. This idea is further supported by a wine cooler or cistern, signed "F.F.F." and dated 1574 now in the Wallace Collection, London (fig. 8). The inside of the cistern reproduces exactly, except for the decorative border, the drawing under consideration as well as that at Windsor.

Because of the late date of the cistern, Gere questions whether the Windsor drawing has anything to do with the Spanish Service (Gere, 1963, p. 313). Oberhuber and Moir have assumed, therefore, that Gere rejects a similar relationship with the present drawing. Oberhuber observes that the red wash technique used also appears in the only surviving drawing for the Spanish Service in the Louvre (6676, ill. in Gere 1969a, pl. 120).

Owing to the substantial difference in the border decoration and the twelve years difference in the date of the paper used for this drawing and the Wallace Collection cistern, a direct relationship between them should be rejected. This is further supported by the second existing drawing at Windsor and the existence of at least nine drawings that relate to the Bargello cistern (and at least two other cisterns in the Prado and the Flint Institute of Arts). The age of the paper, the red wash technique and the general level of quality of the drawing suggest a closer relationship to the Spanish Service. Because it must be assumed that some of the working drawings for the service were delegated to assistants, the attribution of this drawing to the workshop of Taddeo should stand while a substantial level of supervision by the master should also be assumed.

TADDEO ZUCCARO

30 *A Standing Prophet with a Scroll and a Book*

Pen and ink with brown wash over red chalk, squared in charcoal
261 x 141 mm. (10 ⅜ x 5 ½ inches)
The Art Institute of Chicago, Leonora Hall Gurley Memorial Collection,
1922.2965

PROVENANCE: Unidentified collector's mark "PB" surmounted by a crown in red; William F.E. Gurley, Chicago; Leonora Hall Gurley Memorial Collection (Lugt supp. 1230b).

LITERATURE: Gere 1969a, p. 137, no. 21 and p. 80, n. 1; Joachim and McCullagh 1979, p. 37.

EXHIBITIONS: none

This drawing was initially attributed by Ulrich Middeldorf and Federico Zeri to Federico Zuccaro based on similarities with his painted prophets in the chapel at the Villa d'Este at Tivoli. John Gere then correctly assigned the drawing to Taddeo and demonstrated it to be a study for the prophet on the right side wall of the Capella Maggiore in the church of S. Eligio degli Orefici, Rome. The work in this chapel is mentioned in Vasari's life of Taddeo and is assumed to have been executed late in the artist's career and left unfinished at his death because documents of February and June, 1569 mentioned that Federico was paid for additional work (see Gere 1969, p. 137).

30

Clearly, the prototypes for this figure are Taddeo's studies for the prophets on the pilasters of the Frangipani Chapel in S. Marcello al Corso, particularly the drawings in Berlin (Kupferstichkabinett 2677), Munich (Staatliche Graphische Sammlung 37815) and the Metropolitan Museum (cat. no. 21). The figure is more voluminous and somewhat more billowy, however and in spite of the significant water damage on the sheet, a further development of Taddeo's style is evident in the Chicago drawing. An interesting comparison is produced when it is viewed with the drawing of *St. Paul* in the Baltimore Museum (cat. no. 20) where the intensity of Taddeo's conception and execution are more in evidence. The forms in this sheet are more concrete in their realization much in the same fashion as the Berlin *Prophet*.

ATTRIBUTED TO TADDEO ZUCCARO

31 *A Design for an Overdoor Decoration* c. 1564

Pen and ink with brown wash. Watermark: Crossed arrows surmounted by a six-pointed star (similar to Briquet 6291, Rome, 1561-62)
235 x 424 mm. (9 ¼ x 16 ⅝ inches)
Fogg Art Museum, Harvard University, Cambridge, Massachusetts
Bequest of Meta and Paul J. Sachs, 1965.434.

PROVENANCE: Sir Peter Lely (Lugt 2092); John Talman (per Hugh McAndrew); Colnaghi's, London; Paul J. Sachs.

LITERATURE: Mongan and Sachs 1940, no.212, fig.116; Gere 1969a, p.168, under no.108; Lazarus and Yassin 1972-73, p.4, fig.5; Gere and Pouncey 1983, pp.209-210.

EXHIBITIONS: Santa Barbara 1943; Indianapolis 1954, no.40; Cambridge 1962, no.40.

WORKSHOP OF TADDEO ZUCCARO

32 *Study for an Overdoor Decoration* c. 1564

Inscribed in ink lower center: *Pellegrino Tibaldi Bolognese*
Pen and ink with brown wash
240 x 414 mm. (9 ⁷⁄₁₆ x 16 ⁵⁄₁₆ inches)
The University of Michigan Museum of Art, Ann Arbor 1966/1.93

PROVENANCE: collector's mark "F.H."(not in Lugt); Peter Claas, London; sold Sotheby's London 25 March 1965, no.57; Purchased from Mathias Komer, New York.

LITERATURE: St. John Gore, "The London Galleries - Italian Variety," *Apollo*, June, 1965, p.494; Gere, 1969a, p.169, under no. 108; Lazarus and Yassin 1972-73, pp.1-6; Emison 1987, p.32, n.9.

EXHIBITION: *Drawings of Five Centuries...presented by Peter Claas*, Alpine Gallery, London, 1965, no.68, pl.X.

31

32

It is quite clear that the Fogg and Ann Arbor drawings relate to the allegorical figures on the south end wall of the Sala Regia in the Vatican over the door to the Pauline Chapel (fig. 9). Underneath them to either side are *The Siege of Tunis* painted by Taddeo and *Henry IV Submitting to Gregory VII at Canossa*, executed by Federico after Taddeo's death. More vexing are the reasons why these two drawings and those in the British Museum (1947-4-12-154 *verso*, Gere 1969a, pl.158) and in the Biblioteca Reale, Turin (16037) are all similar to one another but contain substantial differences from the final appearance of the fresco.

Gere, Lazarus and Yassin have suggested that these two drawings and the one in Milan were executed by workshop assistants after the British Museum sketch to serve as a model for part of the standard procedure in developing a compositional program. The fact that these drawings are not squared for enlargement suggests that, while the design prototype served a function in the workshop training, it did not survive final scrutiny as the actual execution of the frescoes approached.

Introduced into the evidence is a drawing in the Yale University Art Gallery, previously attributed to Jacopo Bertoia, now given to Raffaellino da Reggio (1961.61.32 ill. in Haverkamp-Begemann and Logan 1970, no.264, pl.146) that accurately depicts the appearance of the left-hand figure, identified as Africa, in the fresco. Its more loosely applied washes, are close to the Ann Arbor drawing, and it might be from the hand of the same artist, although at this point, Raffaellino da Reggio is only a possible solution. The cataloguer in the 1987

fig. 9, Taddeo Zuccaro, *Battle of Tunis and Henry IV Submitting to Gregory VII*, Vatican, Sala Regia

exhibition (Emison 1987, p.30) suggests that the drawing is a copy after the fresco. I would, however, endorse its role as another preliminary stage to the final composition, exhibiting as it does a number of small differences, such as the angle of the pose of the figure, that a copyist would not attempt, as well as a much greater understanding of the psychological state of repose, again not necessarily an issue the copyist would be exploring.

Previously unmentioned is the fact that Taddeo had the opportunity to conceive of the allegory of Africa once before he undertook the decorations for the Sala Regia. Vasari tells us that he executed a series of paintings for the Requiem Mass held in Rome for Emperor Charles V in 1559, which he completed in twenty-five days (Vasari 1850, V, p.190). The subjects of these scenes were published in the early seventeenth century based on descriptions by an anonymous visitor to the obsequies (Berendsen 1970, pp.809-810). Painting number four depicted "Africa, an enormous woman seated on the edge of a boat. Appearing very sad as she leaned on her right hand, she wore a visor designed as an elephant head. At her side were spoils and shields decorated with moons." What follows is an inscription referring to the Battle of Tunis (Berendsen 1970, p.810). Thus, it appears that the experience of designing, albeit rather quickly, these commemorative decorations for Charles V, became useful once more when immediate solutions were required for the end wall of the Sala Regia.

TADDEO ZUCCARO

33 *A Pope Presenting a Standard to a Kneeling Man*
c. 1561-65

Inscribed on mount: *Sebastiano Del Piombo* and on verso: *Original drawing by/ Sebastiano del Piombo./From Wm. Carey's Collection, "53" and "72".*
Pen and ink over black chalk, incised.
283 x 220 mm. (11 ³/₁₆ x 8 ⅞ inches)
Philadelphia Museum of Art, Philadelphia: The Muriel and Philip Berman Gift Acquired from the John S. Phillips bequest of 1876 to the Pennsylvania Academy of Fine Arts, with funds contributed by Muriel and Philip Berman and Edgar Vigues Seeler Fund (by exchange) PAFA-194

PROVENANCE: William Carey, London; John Neagle, Philadelphia.

LITERATURE: Gere 1969a, p. 200, no. 210, pl. 144; Partridge 1978, pp. 504-506.

EXHIBITIONS: *Old Master Drawings from the Academy Collection,* Philadelphia, 4 March-14 April 1974, no. 10; *Old Master Drawings: Museum and Academy Collections,* Philadelphia Museum of Art, 27 Feb.-6 July, 1976.

Gere has pointed out that this drawing is similar in certain aspects of its composition to two scenes from the history of the Farnese family in the Sala dei Fatti Farnesiani at the family's villa at Caprarola, *Paul III Creating Pierluigi Farnese Captain-General of the Church* and *Eugenius IV Creating Ranuccio Farnese Captain-General of the Church*, (cf. Faldi 1981, pp. 148 and 156). A quick sketch for the former painting is included in the present exhibition (cat. no. 38 *verso*) and it is clear that from the outset Taddeo planned the scene as a horizontal composition and not a vertical one and that the striking *repoussoir* element of the soldier in contrapposto on the right side of the drawing was not considered for the scene. The relationship with the latter scene is also not compelling and the overall differences with other known studies for this portion of the Caprarola commission argue against the Philadelphia drawing's role in the Caprarola project. The style of the drawing points more likely to the drawings related to the decoration of the Sala dei Fasti Farnesiani in the Palazzo Farnese (now the French Embassy) in Rome, executed between 1563-65.

Returning to the powerfully built repoussoir figure, it was a device with which Taddeo experimented at the end of his career. (The figure might have been suggested to him by Perino del Vaga's *Story of Alexander* in the Castel S. Angelo of 1545-47). In the British Museum (1946-7-13-108) is a study for the *Donation of Charlemagne* for the Sala Regia of 1564-65, where the same figure is seen in reverse, although he was substantially altered in the final composition of the fresco, particularly the position of the left arm and leg (Gere 1969a, pls. 154

33

and 155). Federico Zuccaro would later adapt this figure to his designs for the *Flagellation* for the fresco in S.Lucia del Gonfalone of 1573 (Uffizi 11029F; Berlin, Kupferstichkabinett, illustrated in Voss, 1920, II, fig. 177). Apparently a popular compositional device with artists working in Rome, it would surface in a slightly altered form in Francesco Vanni's painting of *The Blessed Ambrogio Sansedoni Before the Pope* from the bier of the Company of the Blessed Ambrogio Sansedoni, executed in 1584 and now in a Sienese private collection (illustrated in *L'Arte a Siena sotto i Medici 1555-1609*, Rome, 1980, pp. 127-130).

TADDEO ZUCCARO OR WORKSHOP

34 *The Foundation of Orbetello* c. 1563-65

Pen and ink with brown wash over black chalk, lightly squared for transfer
in black chalk
264 x 392 mm. (10 ⅜ x 15 ⁵⁄₁₆ inches)
Pierpont Morgan Library, New York, The Janos Scholz Collection 1973.27

PROVENANCE: Sir Thomas Lawrence (Lugt 2445); Samuel Woodburn;
Lawrence-Woodburn sale, London, Christie's 4-8 June 1860, part of lot
1074; Sir Thomas Phillipps; his daughter, Mrs. Katharine Fenwick; her son,
T. Fitzroy Phillipps Fenwick; A.S.W. Rosenbach; Janos Scholz.

LITERATURE: Gere 1969a, p.181, no.150, pl.161; Gere 1970, p.127, no.6;
Cheney 1981, no.6, fig.6; Ryskamp 1984, p.188.

EXHIBITIONS: Indianapolis 1954, no.41; Cambridge 1962; Stubbe 1963,
no.179, fig.55; Haverkamp-Begemann and Sharp 1964, no.55; New York,
1965; Houston, 1966, no.55; Providence, 1968, no.vi; Oberhuber and Walker
1973, no.8.

While Taddeo was engaged in the decorative scheme for the villa at
Caprarola, he was given another important domestic commission by
the Farnese, this time by Ranuccio Farnese to complete the
decoration begun by Francesco Salviati in 1549 (and left unfinished at his death
in 1563) in the Sala dei Fasti Farnesiani in the family's Roman palazzo. Like its
analog at Caprarola, the iconographical program was to isolate notable deeds of
the Farnese against the backdrop of mythological and allegorical precedents and
references. The room itself is a mixture of various illusions, feigned tapestries,
pseudo-sculpture, *faux marbre* rivetments, painted medallions and festooned
quadri riportati. Gere (1969a, p.119ff) has brought together the many preliminary
sketches for Taddeo's part in the commission, to which Cheney has added
others.

The Foundation of Orbetello is one of the feigned tapestries above the main door
to the room (fig. 10). It represents the moment in the year 1100 when Pietro
Farnese established the city. The drawing in the Morgan Library was
unenthusiastically accepted by Gere in his catalogue (1969a, p.121) citing "a
certain insipidity in the faces" that contrasts with the strength found in the other
Morgan Library sketch for the six soldiers at the head of Farnese's forces in the
fresco, a group not present in this drawing. Although the participation of
Taddeo's workshop is a possibility in certain of the drawings for the Palazzo

34

fig. 10, Taddeo Zuccaro, *The Foundation of Orbetello*, Palazzo Farnese, Rome

Farnese, it is clear that the drawing under discussion represents an intermediate solution to the composition somewhere between a drawing in the British Museum (1947-4-12-154) and the final fresco. It is quite true to the subsidiary details of the mounted soldiers and the middle and background elements such as the sacrifice that takes place to the left. What is missing are the very physical repoussoir figures in the foreground, suggesting the possibility that Taddeo turned over aspects of the general design to his workshop and then devised the more interesting poses of the foreground figures that serve to activate the somewhat tedious arrangement of the Farnese troops.

TADDEO ZUCCARO

35   *A Group of Warriors* c. 1563-65

Inscribed lower right: Thadeo Z.
Pen and ink with brown wash, squared in chalk
221 x 161 mm. (8 ¾ x 6 ¼ inches)
The Pierpont Morgan Library, New York, The Janos Scholz Collection
1978.1

PROVENANCE: Jonathan Richardson, Sr. (Lugt 2183); Janos Scholz, New York.

LITERATURE: Gere 1969a, p.181, no.151, pl.164; Gere 1970, p.128, no.7; Scholz 1976, no.46; Cheney 1981, no.8, fig.7; Ryskamp 1984, p.223.

EXHIBITIONS: Houston 1966, no.56; Providence 1968, no.V.2; Oberhuber and Walker 1973, no.8; Pignatti 1974, no. 31.

Taddeo Zuccaro's hand is present in every aspect of this particularly strong preparatory sketch for the group of six soldiers in the foreground of the *Foundation of Orbetello* in the Sala dei Fasti Farnesiani at the Palazzo Farnese, Rome (fig. 10). As suggested in the previous entry, it is possible that the group was added by Taddeo in order to improve on the composition sketched by one of his assistants. The difference in scale between the set of figures in each of the two Morgan Library drawings might account in part for the impression of a difference in their general quality.

Also of interest is the very literal rendering of this group in the fresco itself. This supports a dating to the very last moment before the execution of the fresco and might suggest either the *garzone*'s need to follow the master's directions to the letter or, indeed, the active participation of Taddeo in this area of the fresco's execution, the quality of the painting being especially high in the foreground areas.

35

TADDEO ZUCCARO

36 *Cardinal Albornoz Giving the Keys of Valentano to the Farnese* c. 1563-1565

Pen and ink with brown wash over black chalk, squared in red chalk
302 x 275 mm. (11 ⅞ x 10 ⅞ inches)
The J. Paul Getty Museum, Malibu 87.GG.52

PROVENANCE: Giuseppe Vallardi, Milan (Lugt 1223); private collection, Boston; Boston art market.

LITERATURE: Malibu, 1988, p. 174, no. 60.

EXHIBITIONS: none

This previously unknown drawing for the Palazzo Farnese, Rome is a study for the fresco above the right hand side windows in the Sala dei Fasti Farnesiani. The rather obscure subject, identified by Cheney (1981a, p. 261) appears in another study for the fresco in Darmstadt (Hessisches Landesmuseum AE 1562) attributed by Gere to Federico (1969a, no. 26). Gere accepts the Getty drawing as by Taddeo, an opinion which is supportable although the drawing seems stylistically more akin to the *Foundation of Orbetello* (cat. no. 34) than to the *Group of Warriors* (cat. no. 35). There is a marked contrast in regard to style between it and the compositionally related sketch in the Louvre (4462) thought to depict *Guido Farnese Subduing Sedition at Orvieto*, for good reason thought to be a workshop product (Gere 1969b, pp.38-39, no.36, pl.VIII and Cheney 1981b, p.801, no.9).

EXHIBITED IN NEW YORK ONLY

36

TADDEO ZUCCARO

37   *Female Allegorical Figure Seated Next to an Altar*
c. 1563-65

Pen and ink with brown wash heightened with white over black chalk
259 x 324 mm. (10 ⅜ x 12 ½ inches)
Mrs. A. Alfred Taubman, New York

PROVENANCE: Michel Gaud; Sale, Sotheby's, Monaco, 20 June 1987, lot 54.

LITERATURE: none

EXHIBITIONS: none

This previously unknown drawing is a preparatory sketch for one of the female allegorical figures over the windows in the Sala dei Fasti Farnesiani. Though certain changes were made before the fresco was painted, this is surely a very late study by Taddeo. Its broader, more solid forms are those one would expect from figures meant to simulate sculpture as these figures do, and contrast with the other studies for the room that are either for *quadri riportati* or feigned tapestries. Otherwise, the style itself might point to the hand of Federico or one of the workshop assistants involved in the project.

Several studies and versions of the other female allegory, possibly depicting *Valor*, over the right window have been published by Gere (1969a, p.161, no.96) and Cheney (1981b, pp.804-805, nos.15-18). These are a squared version in the British Museum (5211-54), another formerly in the Rosenbach Collection and now temporarily in the collection of the British Rail Pension Fund, a third in the Biblioteca Marucelliana, Florence, on blue paper, a fourth in Berlin (KK 18263) and a fifth in Hanover. All but the British Museum version are considered by Gere to be studio works. The Taubman drawing shares with these sketches the use of wash and white heightening to work out the play of light in a more sculptural manner.

Most of the surviving studies for this project are squared for transfer. Since this one is not and contains some changes from the painted figure, it must be assumed that it represents an alternative not pursued by the artist.

37

TADDEO ZUCCARO

38 *Julius III Restoring the Duchy of Parma to Ottavio Farnese*

verso: *The Marriages of Ottavio Farnese and Margaret of Austria and Orazio Farnese and Diane de Valois; Paul III Creating Pierluigi Farnese Captain-General of the Church*, 1562-63

Inscribed on verso in Taddeo's hand in brown ink: *la prefettura il lume a ma ma[n]cha / il basto[ne] del ducha pier louigi il lume / a ma ma[n]cha/ la legazione del cardinale farnese / in alemagna ed il capita[nato] generale / ...del ducha ottavio / prefettura del duc / la biro del prefeto / il basto[ne] del general / il sposalizio del ducha /il sposalizio del duch,"* and in other hands: *di Taddeo Zuccaro 4.3.* and *D.31 17 20.*
Pen and ink with brown wash over stylus and black chalk. Verso: pen and ink with brown wash over traces of black and red chalk
Watermark: unidentified coat of arms
379 x 559 mm. (14 ¹⁵⁄₁₆ x 22 inches)
The Pierpont Morgan Library, New York, The Janos Scholz Collection
1973.27

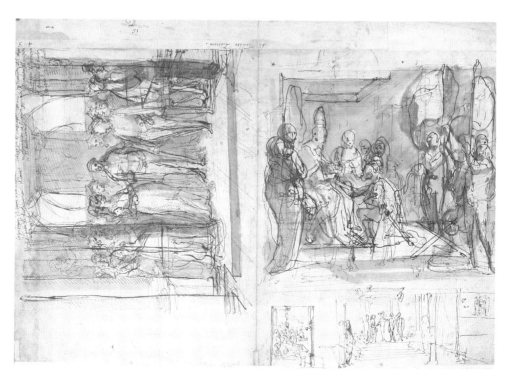

38 verso

38 *recto*

PROVENANCE: William Gibson (?); Jonathan Richardson, Sr. (Lugt 2184); Thomas Dimsdale (Lugt 2426); Sir Thomas Lawrence; Samuel Woodburn; Lawrence-Woodburn sale, London, Christie's, 4-8 June 1860, part of lot 1074; Sir Thomas Phillipps; his daughter Mrs. Katharine Fenwick; her son, T. Fitzroy Phillipps Fenwick; A.S.W. Rosenbach; Janos Scholz.

LITERATURE: Popham and Fenwick 1965, p. 32; Gere 1969a, p. 180, no. 149, pls. 146 and 148; Gere 1969b, p. 38; Gere 1970, p. 127, no. 5, pl. 1; Partridge 1978, pp. 494-529, figs. 22, 27, and 40; Faldi 1981, pp. 52, 56, and 59; Ryskamp 1984, pp. 187-188.

EXHIBITIONS: Staten Island 1961, no. 34; Bean and Stampfle 1965, no. 136; Pillsbury and Caldwell 1966, no. 57; London 1968, no. 116, pl. 11; Middletown 1969, no. 15; Oberhuber and Walker 1973, no. 7.

Since this drawing contains three studies that relate to specific frescoes in the Sala dei Fatti Farnesiani in the Farnese Villa at Caprarola and it carries notations in Taddeo's own hand, it becomes one of the most important documents pertaining to the commission and the artist's involvement with it.

The massive pentagonal villa at Caprarola was begun around 1530 based on designs by Baldassare Peruzzi, Antonio da Sangallo the Younger and, later, by

Jacopo Barozzi da Vignola. Most of the project was completed by Vignola's death in 1573. Around 1562-3, Taddeo Zuccaro began the designs for the Sala dei Fatti Farnesiani. These were followed by those for the Anticamera del Concilio on the *piano nobile* of the villa. The Sala dei Fatti Farnesiani frescoes themselves were executed in the summer of 1563 (Partridge 1978, p. 494, n. 1, 3-5). In 1565, Taddeo received the iconographic program for the Stanza della Solitudine and was helped in the execution of the frescoes by Federico, recently returned from his unsuccessful bid for the decorations of the end wall in the Sala del Gran Consiglio of the Ducal Palace in Venice (see cat. no. 57). During this year the frescoes in the Stanza dell'Aurora and Stanza dei Lanefici were also completed. After Taddeo's death in 1566, Federico continued the decorations, finishing work in the chapel and half the frescoes in the Sala d'Ercole in 1566-67. By 1569, Federico's pace had slackened to the extent that the Cardinal Alessandro Farnese lamented the artist's dilatoriness to his major-domo in Rome, Lodovico Tedeschi (Faldi 1981, p. 31). At this point, other artists were brought in to help finish the work including Jacopo Bertoia, Giovanni de Vecchi and Raffaellino da Reggio.

The Sala dei Fatti Farnesiani, or "Room of Farnese Deeds", is one of the three principle rooms on the *piano nobile* of the villa at Caprarola. It connects, on the lower right arm of the pentagon, the chapel with the Stanza Grande del Consilio and was the principle audience room. The iconographical program, comprised of 27 separate frescoes, was conceived jointly by Cardinal Alessandro Farnese, Paolo Manuzio, a publisher in Rome and Venice, and Onofrio Panvinio, an Augustine historian and antiquarian. Partridge has presented substantial evidence that Panvinio had the major role in conceiving the elaborate program that combines aspects of the family's heraldry and history with political purposes by linking the family with scenes of classical antiquity and the temporal power of the Roman church. The fourteen major moments from the deeds of the Farnese carry identifying inscriptions composed by Manuzio. In his life of Taddeo, Vasari quotes ten of the inscriptions (Vasari, 1850, V, pp. 209-11). A large number of drawings for the room survive, most of which are cited by Partridge and several exist in multiple versions (an addition to Partridge's list is a study, or possibly a copy, of the figure of *Spiritual Sovereignty*, presently on the Munich art market).

The *recto* of the Morgan Library drawing for the fresco on one of the side walls of the room illustrates the moment when, in 1550, Pope Julius III restored the Duchy of Parma to Ottavio Farnese (fig. 11). The restoration of Parma to the Farnese would later incite a war between the forces of the Emperor Charles V, backed by the Pope, and the Farnese, supported by the French. The fresco commemorates the sovereign right, rather than the military might of the

fig. 11, Taddeo Zuccaro, *Julius III Restoring the Duchy of Parma to Ottavio Farnese*, Villa Farnese, Caprarola

victorious Farnese. A fully worked and squared *modello* for the fresco is in the Louvre (RF 1870-73. Several copies of the Louvre drawing exist, one of which is also in the Morgan Library, I.23) There are virtually no differences in the elements included in the Morgan and Louvre drawings although a number of substantive changes were made in the painting. The altar was removed from the background and a number of portraits of the principles were added or their positions were changed. The most important of these was the addition of Prince Alessandro Farnese to the group of Cardinal Farnese and his brother Ottavio who receive the model of the city from Julius. Although Ottavio was only five years old in 1550, he would become the Duke of Parma in 1586 and, thus, represents the aspect of continuity in the family's claim to the duchy.

On the *verso* of the drawing, sketches for two, or as has been argued three, other scenes are depicted. The drawing has traditionally been called *The Marriage Between Orazio Farnese and Diane de Valois*, daughter of King Henry II of France, in 1552 (fig. 12). This marriage is one of two depicted on the end wall of the Sala dei Fatti Farnesiani. The other portrays *The Marriage of Ottavio Farnese and Margaret of Austria*, in 1538. Gere and the Morgan Library have identified the Morgan sketch as the wedding of Orazio, largely owing to the absence of the figure of the Pope in the center (Gere 1969a, p. 180, no. 149 and Ryskamp 1984, p. 187). Partridge (1978, p. 510, n. 74) has suggested the intriguing possibility that the sketch was first designed for the *Marriage of Ottavio*, since it corresponds more closely in pictorial elements and gestures with this fresco than with the other marriage scene. Taddeo then changed the costume of the Pope to accord more with that of Henry II, added the square bases for the columns and used the sketch as a point of departure for the portrayal of Orazio. Drawings in the Louvre (4460) and Chatsworth (736) support this interpretation. Also in support is the curious repeated reference to *il sposalizio del ducha* in the inscription on the drawing.

fig. 12, Taddeo Zuccaro, *The Marriages of Orazio and Ottavio Farnese*, Villa Farnese, Caprarola

The last sketch is for *Paul III Creating Pier Luigi Farnese Captain-General of the Church in 1535*, one of the frescoes on the opposite end wall of the Sala dei Fatti Farnesiani (fig. 13). The primary drawing on this section of the sheet carries underneath it alternate ideas for this scene and that of the Farnese marriages. As with the drawing of the *Restoration of the Duchy of Parma* on the recto, the final appearance of the fresco alters very few elements of the initial sketch. The only major addition was the figure of Pier Luigi's son Ranuccio in the painted version. The subcompartmentalization of this side of the drawing is reminiscent of Taddeo's manner of working found in the drawings for the Frangipani Chapel.

PETRVS · LVISIVS · FARNESIVS ·
A · PAVLO · III · PONTIFICE · MAXIMO ·
ECCLESIASTICI · EXERCITVS · IMPERATOR ·
CONSTITVITVR · ANNO · SAL · OODXXXV ·

fig. 13, Taddeo Zuccaro, *Paul III Creating Pierluigi Farnese Captain-General of the Church*, Villa
Farnese, Caprarola

TADDEO ZUCCARO

39 *The Infant Bacchus Killed by the Titans and Restored to Life by Rhea* c. 1560

Inscribed in Skippe's eighteenth century hand: *Zuccaro*
Pen and ink with brown wash
256 x 256 mm. (10 $\frac{1}{16}$ x 10 $\frac{1}{16}$ inches)
Los Angeles County Museum of Art, Purchased with Funds Provided by
the Dalzell Hatfield Memorial Fund and by Richard G. Benter, M.79,124

PROVENANCE: John Skippe; his descendant J. Rayner-Wood; sale,
Christie's London, 21 November 1958, lot 232a; Lord Brooke, London.

LITERATURE: Gere 1969a, p.170, cat. 116, pl.132 and p.109; Faldi 1981, p.55.

This drawing was used as a preliminary design for one of the frescoed medallions in the Camera dell'Autunno on the ground floor of the Farnese Villa at Caprarola (fig. 14). Both Skippe and Gere have attributed the drawing to Taddeo, but Popham, unaware of its connection with the fresco, gave the sheet to Federico in the catalogue of the Skippe sale. There seems to be no particularly strong evidence of Federico's involvement in this drawing, its distinctly linear treatment meant to be easier for assistants to follow as they translated the design to the fresco stage.

The portrayal of the two titans holding the arms and throat of the young Bacchus suggests that Taddeo was working from the poses of a model seen from both back and front, much as one would find in the work of Antonio Pollaiuolo in Florence in the preceding century.

fig. 14, Taddeo Zuccaro, *The Infant Bacchus Killed by the Titans and Restored to Life by Rhea*, Villa Farnese, Caprarola

39

The subject, though a standard one in classical literature, was not a common one in art. Called the "twice born", Bacchus was born with a horn growing from his head, around which serpents entwined (Taddeo has given him two horns). Hera commanded the Titans to seize him, although he tried to elude them by changing shape. They finally captured him and tore him into pieces which were then boiled in a large cauldron. Rhea, his grandmother, found the remains in the cauldron and restored him to life. Dionysian stories frequently revolve around the idea of death and resurrection and, thus, link his role as a god of vegetation in Greek mythology with the idea of cyclical renewal.

FEDERICO ZUCCARO

40 *Saint John the Baptist*

Inscribed in ink lower left by "Pseudo-Resta": *g 6*
Pen and ink with brown wash over traces of black chalk, area of repair in
lower left.
231 x 175 mm. (9 ⅛ x 6 ⅞ inches)
Duke Roberto Ferretti, Montreal

PROVENANCE: The Pseudo-Resta; Jonathan Richardson, Sr.(Lugt 2184),
mount with shelfmarks V.44/2g.'15/LL.26; sale, Christie's London, 8
December 1981, lot 36.

LITERATURE: none

EXHIBITIONS: none

In a letter dated 19 October 1970, Loren Partridge suggested that this drawing
is a study for the fresco in the chapel at the Farnese villa at Caprarola and
should date, therefore, to around 1566-67. Although there are substantial
differences between the drawing and the painting, the fresco showing the
Baptist full-length without the two bystanders and gesturing upwards, the
subject is rare enough in Federico's *oeuvre* to suggest that it might, at least, be an
early idea for the subject. In Berlin (Kupferstichkabinett 21806) is a sheet of
studies probably for Caprarola that shows the Baptist standing with his arm
raised much in the manner of the Ferretti figure. A seated Baptist in a landscape,
again gesturing heavenward, with a similar staff and lamb and very similar in
terms of style is in Stockholm (Nationalmuseum 448).

In terms of style, the Ferretti drawing is characteristic of Federico's work while
he is still strongly under the influence of Taddeo.

40

FEDERICO ZUCCARO

41 *The Lord Creating the Sun and the Moon* c. 1566-69

Inscribed on mount: *Titian - from vol. 2nd N.15*
Pen and ink with brown wash heightened with white. Watermark: on old
backing papers (now removed) 1. Crown and Star, variant of Briquet 4832-
36 and 4854; 2. Lily, variant of Briquet, 7099-7100, the latter a paper from
Caprarola.
325 x 260 mm. (12 ½ x 10 ¼ inches)
Oberlin College, Allen Memorial Art Museum, Oberlin, Ohio Gift
of Robert Lehman, 47.2

PROVENANCE: Earls of Pembroke, Wilton House; sale, Sotheby's London,
5 July 1917, no.460; Robert Lehman, New York.

LITERATURE: S.A. Strong, *Reproductions of the Old Masters...at Wilton
House*, London, 1900, no.9 (as Titian); Collobi 1938, p.72, pl.40, fig.2;
Stechow 1976, no.370, fig.107; Gere and Pouncey 1983, I, pp.185 and 188.

EXHIBITIONS: Columbus 1961, no.84; Vitzthum 1970, no.12, repr.; Nielson
1971, no.13.

First catalogued as a drawing by Titian while at Wilton House, this drawing
was recognized by Collobi as a study for the central scene on the ceiling of
the chapel at Caprarola (fig. 15). A schematic plan of the ceiling by a
Zuccaro associate named Giovanni Antinor, formerly in the Rosenbach and
British Rail Pension Fund collections, is presently on the art market (fig. 16).

fig. 15, Federico Zuccaro, *The Lord
Creating the Sun and the Moon,* chapel
ceiling, Villa Farnese, Caprarola

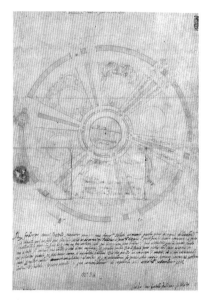

fig. 16, Giovanni Antinor,
*Design for Ceiling of Chapel at the
Villa Farnese, Caprarola,* New
York, art market

41

Despite its water damage, sustained in the last fifty years, this drawing still serves as an excellent example of the close correspondence between Federico's designs for his portions of the decorative campaigns at the Farnese villa and the final product. The only curious change is that from a rectangular composition to a circular one, effected simply by trimming the composition to fit the new format.

The Oberlin drawing is one of Federico's rare homages to the art of Michelangelo. Here he uses as his point of departure the gesture, in reverse, from Michelangelo's fresco of *God Creating the Sun and the Moon* on the Sistine Ceiling.

FEDERICO ZUCCARO

42 Hercules Observing Youths Attempting to Pull his Staff from the Ground, c. 1566-69

Inscribed on verso: *Tadeo Zuccaro 7.1.*
Pen and ink
338 x 270 mm. (13 ¼ x 10 ⅝ inches)
Nissman, Abromson & Co., Brookline, Massachusetts

PROVENANCE: Michel Gaud; sale Sotheby's Monaco, 20 June 1987, lot 24.

LITERATURE: none

EXHIBITIONS: *Italian Drawings*, Nissman, Abromson & Co., New York, 1989, no.3.

Unpublished before its appearance in the Gaud sale, this drawing has, thus far, been universally accepted by all writers on Caprarola and the Zuccari as a design by Federico for the Sala d'Ercole, the loggia in the front side on the *piano nobile* facing the town of Caprarola. Federico worked intermittently on the project between 1566-69, when, owing to a disagreement with Cardinal Alessandro Farnese, he was replaced on the project by Jacopo Bertoia. Federico was only able to complete the large central fresco of *Hercules Swimming in the Lago di Vico* and, according to Partridge (1971, pp.467ff.), a portion of one of the surrounding scenes, *Hercules Plunging his Staff into the Earth*, as well as one of the two lunettes in the room. He was, obviously, thinking ahead for the organization of the ceiling's remaining major narrative moments, *Hercules Watching the Youths Attempting to Pull his Staff from the Earth, Hercules Pulling his Staff from the Earth and the Issuing forth of the Waters*, and *The Peasants Dedicating a Temple to Hercules*. This drawing represents one of the preliminary designs by Federico that were withheld from Bertoia when he assumed the responsibility for the project, Federico not wishing others to benefit from his labors.

The Brookline drawing is filled with gestures and figures typical of Federico. The central figure striding boldly across the center of the composition and gesturing theatrically is familiar from similar figures in *Hercules Swimming in the Lago di Vico*. The use of repoussoir figures is also characteristic as is the appearance of a figure holding on to a tree trunk to get a better view. This type of background character will be frequently found in Federico's urban compositions embracing temple or church columns. Federico's figure of Hercules is a visual quotation of the so-called "Farnese Hercules", the imposing Hellenistic statue found in 1545 in the Baths of Caracalla, and then housed in the Palazzo Farnese,

42

Rome. Hercules's staff is crowned by the Farnese emblem, the *fleur-de-lis*, identifying the hero with Federico's patron.

Not many such unused drawings for the Sala d'Ercole survive by Federico. One such work is found in the British Museum (Gere and Pouncey 1983, no.295).

FEDERICO ZUCCARO

43 *Allegory of Sloth(?)*

Pen and ink with brown wash over black chalk
148 x 212 mm. (5 ³/₁₆ x 8 ⁵/₁₆ inches)
Thomas C. Bartee, on loan to Fogg Art Museum, Harvard University,
Cambridge, Massachusetts 71.1986

PROVENANCE: Count Moriz von Fries, Vienna (Lugt 2903); Jean Willems,
Brussels.

LITERATURE: none

EXHIBITIONS: none

This drawing, previously attributed to Taddeo, should more rightly be given to his brother, Federico. While obscure mythological, historical and religious events appear in Taddeo's oeuvre, allegorical drawings are quite rare, appearing only within the context of palace decorations such as those at Caprarola. This type of imagery is much more in keeping with Federico's interests and judging on style alone the manner of drawing is very much that of Federico, possibly at the time he was working at Caprarola. If one compares the landscape, for example, in the Harvard drawing with his *The Lord Creating the Sun and the Moon* at Oberlin (cat. no. 41) as well as the use of wash, the scales tip in Federico's direction. However, this drawing, like Taddeo's *Saint John the Baptist Preaching* in the Morgan Library (cat. no. 22) also reveals the links connecting the draftmanship of the two brothers. Also close in technical and stylistic terms are the drawings for the Sala de Lanefici at Caprarola (Gere 1969a, pl. 136).

This drawing, thought to depict an allegory of sloth, could well be intended for such a purpose, although such an allegory has not, thus far, been found in the surviving painted decorations for the Farnese villa. It is possible that it is not sloth, however, that is depicted but rather something entirely different. The animal driving the oxcart seems to be the same (a fox?) as that labeled "crass ignorance" in the *Porta Virtutis* at the Morgan Library (cat. no. 85). Thus, the theft of the oxen and cart (symbols of labor) while the owner slumbers, might carry more of a complex moral message than merely a condemnation of laziness.

ATTRIBUTED TO TADDEO ZUCCARO

44 *Study of Three Apostles*

Pen and ink with brown wash, heightened with white, squared in black chalk on brown paper
260 x 203 mm. (10 ¼ x 8 ⅛ inches)
Dr. Carlo M. Croce, Philadelphia

PROVENANCE: Boguslaw Jolles, Dresden and Vienna (Lugt 381); Rudolph Joseph, Munich; sale, Christie's New York, 14 January 1986, lot 4.

LITERATURE: Gere 1969a, p. 147, under no. 52; McTavish, 1985, p. 54 illus.

EXHIBITIONS: none

FEDERICO ZUCCARO

45 *A Group of Apostles*
verso: *The Virgin of the Assumption* c. 1566-68

Pen and ink with brown wash over black chalk, heightened with white incised with stylus. Verso: black chalk
239 x 177 mm. (9 ½ x 7 inches)
Duke Roberto Ferretti, Montreal

PROVENANCE: Albert Wade, London; sale, Christie's London, 11 December 1979, lot 21

LITERATURE: Gere 1966a, p. 293, fig. 18; Gere 1969a, p. 147, under no. 52; *Fine Old Master Drawings*, sale, Christie's New York, 14 January 1986 under no. 4.

EXHIBITIONS: McTavish 1985, no. 20.

44

On 8 June 1563, Taddeo Zuccaro was commissioned to complete the decorations for Cardinal Lorenzo Pucci's chapel in the Roman church of S. Trinità dei Monti at the top of the Spanish Steps. The chapel was originally begun in the 1520's by Perino del Vaga. The actual rights to the chapel were surrendered by the Pucci heirs in 1548 and assumed by the Archbishop of Corfù, Giacomo Caucho who hired Taddeo. The agreement was that the life of the Virgin begun by Perino would be completed with three frescoes, *the Dormition*, *the Assumption*, and *the Sibyl Showing a Vision of the Virgin and Child to the Emperor Augustus*. In addition to this work, a fourth fresco, *God The Father Supporting the Dead Christ, with Angels Holding Instruments of the Passion* was executed. The Pucci Chapel was one of the projects left unfinished upon the death of Taddeo and completed by Federico. The *Assumption* and *Augustus and the Sibyl* are the paintings that demonstrate the most extensive involvement on Federico's part. Gere (1966a) attempts to clarify the respective roles of the two brothers based on a study of the drawings related to the project.

The largest number of extant drawings for the project relate to the *Assumption*. They include first thoughts and more highly finished figure studies by both artists. The Ferretti drawing is a solution for the group of disciples in the lower left of the composition. This figural group would change constantly from one drawing to the next. From the outset it was to contain five figures as evidenced by two drawings in the Uffizi (9342 and 13629) and an engraving made after the drawing by Aliprando Caprioli in 1577. By the time Federico actually painted the fresco, the only figure on that side to remain unchanged was the standing disciple with his hand raised over the sarcophagus. This figure is only lightly sketched in chalk in the Ferretti drawing and articulated more fully in the Croce drawing. The figure on the right of the sheet looking into the empty tomb, originated as a separate figure in a drawing by Taddeo in the Ashmolean, annotated by Federico as the last drawing made by the hand of his brother before his death (Gere 1969a, pl. 175). In the final painting this figure would be changed. The figure of St. James the Great on the left of the Ferretti drawing was introduced by Federico rather late in the development of the composition. He does not appear in the "missing link" drawing in the Croce Collection yet does turn up in the fresco with his arm extended and eyes directed at St. Peter and not at the Virgin. The pose of the kneeling figure who makes eye contact with the viewer in both the Ferretti and Croce drawings was entirely changed in the fresco.

45 *recto*

The relationship between the Ferretti and Croce drawings and the painting of *The Assumption* is made even more complicated by a drawing, unquestionably by Federico, in the Codice Resta in the Biblioteca Ambrosiana (fig. 17). The drawing depicts Christ's *Ascension* and incorporates not only the figure of St. James the Great as he appears in the Ferretti drawing but also the kneeling figure mentioned above who gestures across his body with the right hand to invoke the viewer in both drawings. These elements were altered substantially in the Pucci Chapel fresco. Does this indicate that Federico considered another subject for the painting at one point? To this question, the answer must be negative because the Pucci Chapel was dedicated to the Assumption of the Virgin. Perhaps the Milan drawing simply utilized the discarded solution for the left hand group of Apostles as a component for another commission altogether? While there is no documentation to suggest that Federico ever painted an *Ascension*, this explanation is the most compelling. A third less likely possibility is that the Ferretti and Croce drawings were not intended as preparatory to the Pucci Chapel in the first place.

The *verso* of the Ferretti drawing depicts a seated study for the Virgin with hands clasped. While this might represent the original solution for Mary in the Pucci Chapel *Assumption*, she later evolved into a figure with arms stretched out. Another possibility is that she is a preliminary study for the Virgin in the *Coronation* altarpiece by Federico in S. Lorenzo in Damaso (see cat. no. 61), yet another commission given to Taddeo and left unfinished at his death. A drawing in the Uffizi (9342S), given to Taddeo, also has sketches for the Pucci Chapel and S. Lorenzo altarpiece on *recto* and *verso*.

As regards the attribution of the Croce drawing to Taddeo, it has been accepted by Gere but given the number of alterations in drawings for this commission attributable to Federico, particularly as the figures were beginning to be more fully realized, his responsibility for this drawing should not be ruled out entirely.

fig. 17, Federico Zuccaro, *Ascension of Christ*, Ambrosiana, Milan

45 *verso*

FEDERICO ZUCCARO

46 *The Assumption of the Virgin* c. 1589

Pen and ink with brown wash over black chalk
388 x 523 mm. (15 ¼ x 20 ½ inches)
Collection of the Mackenzie Art Gallery, Regina, Saskatchewan, Gift of Mr.
Norman Mackenzie, 35-7

PROVENANCE: William Mayor, London (Lugt 2799); Norman Mackenzie.

LITERATURE: Vitzthum 1969, p.93.

EXHIBITIONS: Vitzthum 1970, no.14; Alasko 1983, no. 49.

One of a number of sketches by Federico after designs by Taddeo for the altarpiece in the Pucci Chapel, S. Trinità dei Monti, Rome (fig 18). The commission was given to Taddeo in 1563 and completed by Federico in 1589 (see cat. nos. 44 and 45).

It is Gere's opinion that Federico altered the composition substantially, particularly the upper portion where the Virgin is carried aloft by a multitude of putti (Gere 1966, p.293). This might have been introduced by Federico after having seen Titian's great altarpiece of the same subject in the Church of the Frari, Venice. While this is possible, and the Mackenzie drawing certainly has many of the attributes of Federico's hand, its closest related study in Stockholm (442, illustrated in Gere 1966a, fig. 14) has so many aspects of Taddeo's style,

fig. 18, Federico Zuccaro,
Assumption of the Virgin, Pucci
Chapel, S. Trinità dei Monti, Rome

46

especially his electric use of line, that it is difficult to assign the Stockholm sheet, as Gere does, to Federico. If the Stockholm drawing is by Taddeo, it is possible that Federico worked from it to fashion the Mackenzie sheet, just as he did for other parts of the composition. After all, it seems that Taddeo had already made the transition from portraying the Virgin with her hands spread wide, rather than held in prayer, as evidenced by the quick sketch in the Louvre (RF 1870-29242).

Other drawings related to the *Assumption* include those in the Ferretti Collection, the Ashmolean at Oxford (see Parker 1972, II, no.762) and a lost drawing once in the Instituto Jovellanos de Gijon (Perez Sanchez 1969, no. 229, pl. 263). The Uffizi (13629 by Federico after Taddeo) has yet another drawing of which there is a copy in the Wadsworth Atheneum.

FEDERICO ZUCCARO

47 *Apollo and the Muses with Pegasus*

Pen and ink with brown wash over red chalk
243 x 381 mm. (9 ½ x 15 inches)
The Ackland Art Museum, University of North Carolina at Chapel Hill,
63.23.1

PROVENANCE: Schaeffer Galleries, Inc., New York; acquired 1963.

LITERATURE: none

EXHIBITIONS: Chapel Hill 1969, no. 98 (as Cavaliere d'Arpino); Rutgers 1984 (as attributed to Federico Zuccaro).

Purchased as a drawing by the Cavaliere d'Arpino, the attribution to Federico was made by Philip Pouncey and later seconded by Konrad Oberhuber, who subsequently had misgivings. The scratchy penmanship of this work indicates Federico's early style of the late 1550's when he was still under the tutelage of his brother. This dating is supported by circumstantial evidence regarding a pair of commissions dating from these years.

In 1559, Taddeo Zuccaro painted a fresco of the *Apollo and the Muses on Mount Parnassus* in the now demolished casino of the Palazzo Bufalo, Rome. The fresco, though detached, still survives (cf. Gere 1969a, pl. 109.) in a private collection. Vasari tells us (1850, vol. V, p. 189) that at about the same time Taddeo gave the young Federico the opportunity to execute by himself a *Parnassus* in the house of Stefano Margani at the foot of the Capitoline hill.

47

Gere was able to locate one drawing for the Palazzo Bufalo and one copy of a lost drawing, both in the Louvre (Gere 1969a, no. 170, pl. 110 and no. 199). There is also a drawing for the figure of Apollo in the Uffizi that he attributes to Federico (10988F) that is certainly a study for the Palazzo Bufalo and presumably by the hand of Taddeo. The style of the former drawing has nothing in common with the present sheet. While the Ackland drawing does not place Apollo standing in the center of the composition and introduces the winged horse Pegasus, the two compositions are similar in the number of figures around the god (ten) and their division into two wedge-shaped groups on either side of the composition. Given that both brothers were busy with the same theme at roughly the same time, it is logical to deduce that the Ackland drawing could well be an idea for the Margani commission based on Taddeo's own ideas.

This idea gains some support in a drawing for a portion of a wall and ceiling decoration in Munich (34025) that includes a design for a *quadro riportato*, or feigned picture, of Apollo and the Muses with Pegasus among other designs (fig.

19). This sketch is superficially close to the Ackland's drawing. The Munich drawing also includes in reverse, two coats of arms, one that of Pius V (1566-72) and the second those of Michele Bonelli, created cardinal by Pius V in 1566. If the two drawings are related, it would suggest that either the dating of the Margani commission is later than Vasari indicates or that the Chapel Hill drawing is connected with another decorative scheme.

fig. 19, Federico Zuccaro, *Design for a Ceiling*, Staatliche Graphische Sammlung, Munich

A drawing attributed to Federico sold at Christie's (6 July 1976, lot 28) might also be related to the plans for this commission (fig. 20). Also stylistically, as well as somewhat thematically, related to the Ackland drawing is a sketch presently attributed to Taddeo, but formerly to Federico, of *The Choice of Hercules* at the art museum at Bowdoin College (1811.62). A third related idea for the Parnassus theme survives in a copy at Princeton (cat. no. 92).

fig. 20, Federico Zuccaro, *Parnassus* (?), location unknown

FEDERICO ZUCCARO

48 *The Vision of Saint Eustace* 1558-59

Brush with brown, gray, green, yellow, and red wash, heightened with
white, over traces of red and black chalk. Lightly squared in black chalk.
340 x 202 mm. (13 ⅜ x 8 inches)
Metropolitan Museum of Art, New York, Rogers Fund 62.76

PROVENANCE: Jonathan Richardson (Lugt 2184); Jonathan Richardson, Jr.
(Lugt 2170); Sir Joshua Reynolds (Lugt 2364); purchased in London in 1962.

LITERATURE: Bean 1963, p. 232, fig. 5; Gere 1963, p. 394, note 12; Gere
1966, p. 27 under no. 29; Gere 1971, pl.xviii; Smith 1977, pp. 29-30, fig. 37;
Bean 1982, no. 273.

EXHIBITIONS: Bean and Stampfle 1965, no. 140; Olzewski 1981, no. 81.

The drawing carries an extensive inscription in the hand of Jonathan
Richardson on the old mount that is transcribed in the Metropolitan
Museum's catalogue (Bean 1982, no. 273).

The Vision of Saint Eustace is one of the earliest and most fully worked
drawings that survive by Federico while he is still working fully under the
influence of his brother in Rome. Vasari tells us that Taddeo procured for his
eighteen year-old brother the commission to decorate the exterior of the house of
Tizio da Spoleto, Master of the Household of Cardinal Alessandro Farnese. The
small palace on the Piazza Sant' Eustachio still stands and bears traces of the
fresco between the windows on the upper storey (fig. 21). It was part of a

fig. 21, Federico Zuccaro,
House façade with scenes from the life of St. Eustace,
Piazza S. Eustachio, Rome

48

sequence of scenes from the life of the saint including his baptism and martyrdom. It has been noted by Gere and others, that Federico goes beyond the somewhat monochromatic approach to facade decoration made popular by Polidoro da Caravaggio in his use of additional colors in the Metropolitan's drawing.

Vasari further reports that an altercation ensued when Federico took offense at Taddeo's attempts to improve the results of the painted façade and an understanding was reached that "Taddeo might correct or retouch the designs or cartoons of Federico" but not alter the paintings.

Thus, the door is left open in this particular case to find what might possibly be direct influence or even something of the hand of Taddeo in the full corporeality of the saint's pose of surprise, not unlike that of Taddeo's proconsul in the *Blinding of Elymas* from the previous year (cat. no. 15). Regardless of the degree of direct or indirect involvement, in the *Vision of Saint Eustace* one also receives the impression in the soft use of colored washes, of Federico Barocci's immanent presence on the Roman art scene.

A smaller (213 x 138 mm.) related drawing in pen and wash, also squared in black chalk, is in the Uffizi (11173F). The entire scene was engraved by Cherubino Alberti in 1575 (Bartsch XVII, no. 52.)

EXHIBITED IN NEW YORK ONLY

FEDERICO ZUCCARO

49 *Two Studies of a Standing Male Figure in Cloak with Outstretched Arm* c. 1562-3

Inscribed upper right in ink: *46*
Black chalk with blue wash
350 x 250 mm. (13 ¾ x 9 ⁹⁄₁₆ inches)
Margot Gordon, Marcello Aldega, New York

PROVENANCE: Filippo Baldinucci; F.M.N. Gaburri, Florence.

LITERATURE: none

EXHIBITIONS: Aldega, M. and Gordon, M. *Italian Drawings of the XVI Century*, New York, 1987, no. 17.

49

Between June and October 1563 Federico received payment for painting sixteen frescoes from the life of Moses in the Vatican Belvedere commissioned by Pope Pius IV. This drawing is a study for the figure of Moses in one of those scenes, *Moses and Aaron Before Pharaoh* (fig. 22). It can also be compared with the figure of Moses in the *Crossing of the Red Sea* from the same series (see Smith, 1977, fig. 82).

Very few preparatory drawings survive for these paintings and the Gordon/Aldega drawing is unique, so far as can be determined, in Federico's work in its use of blue wash. This particular use of wash and line has a smokiness to it reminiscent of the drawings of Ferrau Fenzoni. A drawing of the entire composition exists in the Louvre (4397) and Gere (1969b, pp.44-45) hints at the likelihood that Federico was helped along by Taddeo in this first large commission by being supplied with some drawings by the elder brother and, perhaps, (echoing an opinion of Körte) correcting other designs by Federico. No such drawings survive, however.

The Belvedere frescoes are among Federico's least satisfying painted works, only achieving a certain level of distinction when he is quoting directly from influential works by his brother, particularly the paintings in the Frangipani Chapel. The entire composition of *Moses and Aaron Before Pharaoh* was engraved in 1567 by Cornelis Cort (Bierens de Haan 1948, no. 18).

fig. 22, Federico Zuccaro,
Moses and Aaron Before Pharoah,
Vatican City, Museo Gregoriano Etrusco

FEDERICO ZUCCARO

50 *Three Studies of the Head of a Bald Bearded Man from Different Viewpoints* c. 1563

Black, red and white chalk on blue prepared paper
192 x 162 mm. (7 ½ x 6 ⅜ inches)
The Art Museum, Princeton University, Princeton, Gift of Frank Jewett
Mather, Jr. 47-122

PROVENANCE: John Rutson, Nunnington Hall, Yorkshire (Lugt 1517);
Frank Jewett Mather, Jr. (Lugt 1853a).

LITERATURE: Scholz 1967, p. 294 (as Ambrogio Figino); Gibbons 1977, no. 701.

EXHIBITIONS: Staten Island 1958, no. 13 (as Bassano); Bean 1966, no. 21.

The attribution to Federico was first suggested by Philip Pouncey. While Jacob Bean concurred (1966, no. 21), the authorship is not unquestioned.

The use of the three colored chalks on blue paper is unusual, although not unprecedented, in Federico's work, therefore making analogies more difficult. It would seem to stem from the years when he and Taddeo were interacting stylistically with Federico Barocci (1561-63). Federico did much experimenting with drawing materials while designing the sixteen scenes from the life of Moses for the Vatican Belvedere. Most of the surviving drawings are in different colored chalks on colored papers. In fact, the face of the man in three quarter view in the Princeton drawing might have been used as a model for the figure of the Pharaoh in the *Plague of the Frogs* (fig. 23). Simultaneously, there is a resemblance between the head of Pharaoh in the *Plague of the Flies* (fig. 24) and the studies in lost profile.

While there is something of a static quality to the drawing that is not entirely typical of Federico's work, the studies made from different points of view seem appropriate to his early work. Thus, the present attribution should be retained.

50

fig. 23, Federico Zuccaro, *The Plague of Frogs*,
Vatican City, Museo Gregoriano Etrusco

fig. 24, Federico Zuccaro, *The Plague of Flies*,
Vatican City, Museo Gregoriano Etrusco

171

FEDERICO ZUCCARO

51 *Three Studies of a Bearded Man*

Inscribed upper left in brown ink: *no. 35*
Red and black chalk
110 x 157 mm. (4 ⅜ x 6 inches)
Rusty Lemorande, Los Angeles

PROVENANCE: Purchased from Spencer Samuels, New York

LITERATURE: *Art and Auction*, November, 1985, p. 60, repr.

EXHIBITIONS: none

This drawing, with its characterizations of a single elderly model seen from three viewpoints, is likely to be, as was the preceding drawing, in preparation for the sixteen scenes from the life of Moses that Federico executed in the Belvedere of the Vatican in 1563. The type of physiognomy is that of a number of the bystanders in the frescoes.

FEDERICO ZUCCARO

52 *Two Male Figures for the Conversion of Mary Magdalene* c. 1563-64

Inscribed lower right in Crozat's hand: *61* and *Taddeo Zucchero*; on lower right of mat: *S E: R.O.X.*
Black chalk with pen and ink and brown wash on blue-green paper
366 x 144 mm. (14 ⁵⁄₁₆ x 5 ¹¹⁄₁₆ inches)
Yale University Art Gallery, New Haven, Everett V. Meeks, B.A. 1901, Fund
1965.9.15

PROVENANCE: Pierre Crozat, Paris (Lugt 2951); Earl of Northwick; his son Edward George Spencer-Churchill; sale, Sotheby's London, 1-4 November, 1920; acquired from Faerber and Maison, Ltd., London in 1965.

LITERATURE: *Yale University Art Gallery Bulletin*, XXXI, no.1, 1966, p.17; Haverkamp-Begemann and Logan 1970, I, p. 156, no. 278 and II, pl.145; Pillsbury 1974, pp.8-10; Harprath 1977, pp. 167-68.

EXHIBITIONS: Vitzthum 1970, no.11, repr.; Pillsbury and Caldwell 1974, no.35 repr.

While assisting Taddeo with the early decorations for the Farnese villa at Caprarola, Federico Zuccaro was summoned to Venice by Cardinal Grimani in November of 1563. A few small decorations were executed in the Palazzo Grimani before Federico turned his attentions to creating a pair of frescoes in the Grimani Chapel in the church of S.Francesco della Vigna whose decoration had been begun by Battista Franco (see Rearick, 1958). Federico executed frescoes of the *Resurrection of Lazarus* and the *Conversion of Mary Magdalene*, the latter painting now lost, a victim of the pervasive dampness of Venice.

The Yale drawing is a fine preparatory study for the two figures at the far left of the *Conversion of Mary Magdalene*. As I have pointed out elsewhere in this catalogue, drawings such as this were probably not made from studio models but served as a template of sorts for the actual studies from life represented, in the case of the man with the turban, in the drawing in the Morgan Library (cat. no. 53 verso). The chalk study published by Pillsbury (1974, fig. 2), once in the Rosenbach Foundation in Philadelphia and presently on the art market is likely a copy (fig. 25). Although it contains variations on the poses in the fresco which suggest the artist working out the compositional problems, its style, particularly the overly mannered heads suggest another hand altogether.

173

fig. 25, Federico Zuccaro,
Study for the Conversion of the Magdalen,
art market, New York

Federico, who had a penchant for self-quotation, would re-utilize this figure in the left foreground of another of his paintings, *The Healing of the Blind Man*, in the Orvieto Cathedral, dated 1568.

A large number of related drawings and copies for the *Conversion of Mary Magdalene* survive. Two are in the Uffizi (1093 and 1097); Munich, Kupferstichkabinett (88, a copy, another version once in the Herbert List and Wolfgang Ratjen Collections was sold London, Christie's, 5 July 1988, lot 37a); Vienna, Albertina (Stix and Fröhlich-Bum, 515, a copy); New York, Pierpont Morgan Library 1974.24); Paris, Louvre (4413); Milan, Castello Sforzesco (942/6971); Truro, Royal Institution of Cornwall (modello); New York, Art Market (ex-Rosenbach Library and British Rail collections, probable copy); a copy of the total composition once Marcello Guidi Collection (whereabouts unknown); Ragghianti, 1974, p. 148 mentions a copy at Lulworth (Weld Collection) retouched by Rubens in the opinion of Michael Jaffé. The entire composition was engraved by Aliprando Caprioli.

FEDERICO ZUCCARO

53 *Studies of Two Boys, Two Arms* c. 1564
verso: *Half-Length Figure of a Man Seen from the Back, and Detail of Left Arm*

Inscribed verso, lower center: *Feder Zuccheri*
Red and black chalk
144 x 207 mm. (5 9/16 x 8 1/8 inches)
The Pierpont Morgan Library, New York, The Janos Scholz Collection
1974.24

PROVENANCE: Giovanni Piancastelli; Edward and Mary Brandegee, Brookline, Massachusetts; Janos Scholz, New York

LITERATURE: Pillsbury 1974, pp.9-10, repr.; Ryskamp 1984, p.186; Wegner 1984, p. 11, note 11.

EXHIBITIONS: Oberhuber and Walker 1973, no. 9, repr.

Pillsbury was the first to point out that both sides of this sheet probably relate to the *Conversion of Mary Magdalene* in the Grimani Chapel, S. Francesco della Vigna in Venice. This is particularly true of the *verso* study of the man seen from behind that is clearly preparatory to the figure wearing the turban on the left of the composition as evidenced by the Yale University drawing (see preceding entry). The purpose of the studies of the youths is less clear although Federico employed similar figures in the proposed compositions for both the *Conversion* and *Raising of Lazarus*.

53 verso

53

A comparison of the Morgan Library sheet and that at Yale provides the perfect opportunity to compare Federico's drawing style in chalks and pen and ink in the same year. The spontaneity of the chalk manner is readily apparent while at this early stage in his career his method in pen and ink tends to be more volumetric and solidly defined. It is this type of draftmanship that supports previous attributions to Federico of the drawing of *Saint Paul* in the Baltimore Museum of Art (cat. no. 20).

FEDERICO ZUCCARO

54 *A Pope Receiving an Emperor on the Steps of a Church*, c. 1563-65

Inscribed lower right, in pencil: c 30
Red and black chalk
336 x 228 mm. (13 ¼ x 9 inches)
The Pierpont Morgan Library, New York, The Janos Scholz Collection
1983.68

PROVENANCE: Possibly Padre Sebastiano Resta (see Lugt 2992); John Lord Somer? (see Lugt 2981); Jean-Denis Lempereur, Paris (Lugt 1740); Sir Thomas Lawrence (Lugt 2445); Samuel Woodburn; Lawrence-Woodburn sale, Christie's, London 4-8 June 1860 part of lot 1074; Sir Thomas Phillipps (see Lugt supp. 924b); his daughter, Mrs. Katharine Fenwick; her son T. Fitzroy Fenwick; A.S.W. Rosenbach, Philadelphia; John Fleming, New York; Janos Scholz

LITERATURE: Gere 1970, p.131, no.20, pl.13; Majeska 1980, pp. 63,76, n.40; Held 1981, p.177; Ryskamp 1984, p.318.

EXHIBITIONS: Oakland 1959, no.83, repr.;Pignatti 1974-75, no.31 (with incorrect measurements).

The composition of the Morgan Library drawing appears in two other drawings as E. Tietze-Conrat has demonstrated, one, in the Uffizi (1828F) and one in the Oppé collection, London. The scene corresponds with descriptions of Tintoretto's *Coronation of Frederick Barbarossa*, executed between 1562-64 for the Sala del Gran Consiglio in the Doge's Palace, Venice and destroyed during the great conflagration of 1577. The style, however, is entirely Federico Zuccaro's and the occasional "improvement" in his copy, might account for Resta's notation regarding this drawing that it seemed "in competition with Paolo Veronese".

Federico made his first trip to Venice in 1563-65 to undertake the decoration of the Grimani Chapel in S. Francesco della Vigna among other projects. Therefore, the timing would have been right for him to make a copy of Tintoretto's recently completed work for the Doge's Palace. Never one to shrink from copying another artist's work in order to broaden his own horizons, Federico here demonstrates his delight in suffusing himself in the Venetian grand manner of the mid-sixteenth century.

The lessons learned by Federico by copying Tintoretto's work would, ironically, be employed in the 1580's when he would have the chance to include certain details in his painting of *The Submission of the Emperor Frederick Barbarossa* made to replace Titian's of the same subject which had perished together with Tintoretto's compositions during the 1577 fire.

54

FEDERICO ZUCCARO

55 *The Holy Trinity and Four Angels* c. 1563

Pen and ink with brown wash, heightened with white on faded blue paper;
lightly squared for transfer
325 x 256 mm. (12 ¾ x 10 inches)
Museum of Fine Arts, Boston, Otis Norcross Fund, 1964.2180

PROVENANCE: Mrs. G. Small

LITERATURE: Gere 1969a, p.125, note 1; Pillsbury 1974, p.13, fig. 18;
Macandrew 1983, no.25.

EXHIBITIONS: Colnaghi's, London, *Old Master Drawings*, June-July, 1964,
no.2; Providence 1968, p.44 and pl. 23, no.2; Boston 1987, 4b.

This is a rare example of Federico working from a German print source for his inspiration. The drawing is a free copy of the 1511 woodcut by Albrecht Dürer (fig. 26). While Federico was not reluctant to incorporate the ideas of other Italian artists into his work, this example of looking to a Northern source is more unusual. It is possible that his experiences in Venice, a city with both a strong German community and greater familiarity with the art of Dürer and his contemporaries, might have influenced his choice of a source. Pillsbury has made a convincing case for Federico's *Dead Christ Supported by an Angel* in the Yale University Art Gallery (cat. no. 56) issuing as well from the Venetian period. It is a work that is linked compositionally to the Boston sheet and, hence, to the Dürer woodcut.

fig. 26, Albrecht Dürer, *The Holy Trinity*,
Museum of Fine Arts, Boston, Bequest of Francis Bullard

55

Federico found the pose of God the Father and Christ to be of greatest interest. His purpose in copying this motif is not clear, however. An effort to connect the drawing with the work done by Federico and Taddeo in S. Trinità dei Monti is not convincing (see Providence, 1968, p.44). The Boston *Trinity*'s relationship to the Yale drawing is, nevertheless, tangible and draws it into a sequence of related works including the painting by Taddeo in the Borghese Gallery (fig. 47) and its replica in the chapel at Caprarola (see Faldi 1981, p.119).

Other related drawings are in Ottawa (6572 O.272), the Uffizi (92139), and the Louvre (4430).

FEDERICO ZUCCARO

56 *Dead Christ Supported by Angels* c. 1563

Inscribed in pen lower right: *Federigo Zuccaro*
Red chalk, Watermark: Anchor inscribed within a circle surmounted by a
star (Briquet 485), Padua, 1547.
347 x 265 mm. (13 ½ x 10 ½ inches)
Yale University Art Gallery, New Haven, Everett V. Meeks B.A. 1901 Fund,
1972.94

PROVENANCE: Acquired in 1972 from H. Shickman Gallery, New York.

LITERATURE: Pillsbury 1974, pp.8-13.

EXHIBITIONS: Pillsbury and Caldwell 1974, no. 34, repr.; Olzewski 1981,
no.78, repr.

Edmund Pillsbury has nicely outlined the place of this drawing within the output of Federico's early works and makes a successful argument for considering it a drawing made during Federico's first trip to Venice around 1563. Pillsbury relates it to other drawings made for his early Venetian commissions, the *Resurrection of Lazarus* and *Conversion of the Magdalene* for the Grimani Chapel and a sheet of studies in the Uffizi (2607S). Other evidence cited in support of a Venetian period origin is the Paduan watermark on the paper.

As cited in the previous entry, the Yale drawing is also related to the drawing of *The Trinity* in Boston and its source in the Dürer woodcut of 1511. The direct or indirect influence of the work of Michelangelo has been suggested as an influence on this composition. While not ruling this out of the question, Federico was seemingly less enamored of Michelangelo than was his brother. If there is any influence here at all to be traced, it may be through the intermediary of Taddeo's own work such as the *Dead Christ* in the Borghese gallery, copied by Federico for the altarpiece in the chapel at Caprarola (fig. 47).

One possible influence on Federico's conception of Christ carried aloft in this manner that has not been mentioned is Titian's *Assumption of the Virgin* in the church of the Frari in Venice, executed between 1516-18. Federico probably derived from Titian's altarpiece his use of the slight diagonal composition, the mild serpentine configuration of Christ as well as the buoyant *putti* seeming to hold the cloud bank in the air.

While the exact purpose of the Yale sketch has not been determined, it was probably an idea for an altarpiece, judging from the quick pen and wash study of an elaborated version of the composition in Budapest (1928), which is shaped in the large vertical *pala* format of the Frari altarpiece, for example. Other related drawings are in the Uffizi (11133 and 813) and Ottawa (6572 O.272).

Federigo Ruetato

56

FEDERICO ZUCCARO

57 *Paradise* c. 1564-1582

Inscribed in pencil on recto lower left: *Taddeo Zucchero* and on verso:
Taddeo Zucchero/Design for a Cieling [sic] for the Cathedral at Urbino
Pen and ink with brown gray, gray-green and red wash, heightened with
white. Left and central sections squared in red chalk. Application of a
separate sheet depicting the Deësis at a later date by the artist.
398 x 1136 mm. (15 ½ x 44 ¾ inches). Addition 140 x 240 mm.
Metropolitan Museum of Art, New York, Rogers Fund 61.201

PROVENANCE: Pierre Crozat (?); sale Paris 10 April - 13 May, 1741,
possibly part of lot 216; Baron von Stumm (according to Voss); purchased,
Munich, 1961.

LITERATURE: Voss 1954, pp. 172-175, fig. 17; Vitzthum 1954, p. 291;
Heikamp 1958, p. 47, note 8; Heikamp 1967, p. 65, note 21; Gere 1969b, pp.
46-47 (no. 49); Tolnay 1970, pp.105-110, fig. 137; Sinding-Larsen 1974, p. 61,
pl. XLIV; Schulz 1980, pp. 112-126, fig. 7; Bean 1982, no. 276.

EXHIBITIONS: none

During Federico's first trip to Venice in 1563-66, we are told by Vasari
that, after completing the Grimani Chapel, he "was on the point of
making an agreement to paint the principal façade in the Hall of the
Grand Council,...But the rivalry and contentions, established on this occasion by
the painters of Venice, prevented Federico from receiving that commission." He
goes on to state that the jealous artists were not able to garner the commission
for themselves, either (Vasari 1850 V, p. 200). The major wall of the Sala del Gran
Consiglio was decorated with a fresco of *Paradise* by Guariento dating from the
1360's and, probably owing to its state of conservation, was a candidate for
replacement. Before any resolution could be agreed upon regarding the artist to
take on the large project, the issue was mooted by the large fire that destroyed
the paintings in the chamber in 1577. A proper competition in 1582 involved
Federico Zuccaro, Palma Giovane, Veronese, Francesco Bassano and Tintoretto
with Tintoretto emerging victorious and completing the painting in 1588.

It is likely that this drawing and one in the Louvre (4546) portraying an earlier
idea, with the *Coronation of the Virgin* in the center rather than the Deësis, were
conceived and executed while Federico was negotiating for the Ducal Palace
commission around 1564. When the 1582 competition took place, Federico re-
submitted the entire project. Schulz (1980, p. 117 and note 33) has demonstrated,

using a novel proportional comparison between the various sketches submitted by the artists and the percentage of the wall height the designs would cover, that Federico's projects were geared to the size of the wall covered by the Guariento fresco rather than the size envisioned after the fire.

The apparent total lack of preliminary drawings for single figures for this composition is intriguing. The only exception can be found in a drawing of a nude seen from behind (Florence, Uffizi 11101F) which resembles closely the figure of Adam in the right central portion of the Metropolitan Museum's *modello*. It lends some credence to the theory that Federico made his overall composition first, then posed studio models in a fashion already dictated by the general scheme, rather than making use of many studies of models in compiling his general composition. A painting of *Paradise* (now lost) is mentioned in the inventories of Francesco Maria II della Rovere's villa at Monte Berticchio (Eiche 1984, pp. 77-108).

EXHIBITED IN NEW YORK ONLY

FEDERICO ZUCCARO

58 *Study of a Seated Youth* c. 1568

Black and red chalk. No watermark visible.
240 x 190 mm. (9 ½ x 7 ½ inches)
Mr. and Mrs. R. Fraser Elliott, Toronto

PROVENANCE: unknown

LITERATURE: none

EXHIBITIONS: Vitzthum 1970, no. 13, repr.; McTavish 1981-82, no. 30, repr.

Previously unrecognized, this drawing is a preparatory sketch for the *Raising of the Son of the Widow of Nain* in the Orvieto cathedral (fig. 27). The altarpiece was commissioned on 14 November 1568 and erected in the second chapel on the left of the nave (L. Fumi, *Il Duomo di Orvieto e suoi restauri*, Rome 1891, p. 416, doc. cxviii). The painting and its companion, *Christ Healing the Blind Man* are now in the Museo dell' Opera del Duomo at Orvieto (Garzelli 1972, pp. 21-22). The Toronto drawing is the only surviving study for the figure of the son brought back to life by Christ (Luke 7:11-16).

The drawing is characteristic of the chalk style of Federico and demonstrates his manner of working from the studio model. Relatively little has changed from the drawing of this figure to the finished painting, beyond the appearance that the young man is resting less upright in the painting.

The composition was engraved by Jacob Matham (fig. 28, B.III, no.233). Other drawings related to this commission are found in Amsterdam (Rijksmuseum A2188), Berlin (Kupferstichkabinett, 18500, 18501 and 18502), London (British Museum 1895-9-15-573 and British Rail Pension Fund Collection, ex-Rosenbach Foundation 128), Paris (Institut Néerlandais 1975-T.12), and Vienna (Albertina 613). Two additional copies of figures are also in Vienna (Albertina 649 and 652). A *modello* probably for the Matham print resides in the Louvre (4525) and a copy of the entire composition is in the Yale University Art Gallery in New Haven (1961.66.16). Of the related drawings only the Toronto sheet and the ex-Rosenbach drawing are in chalk and are studies for single figures.

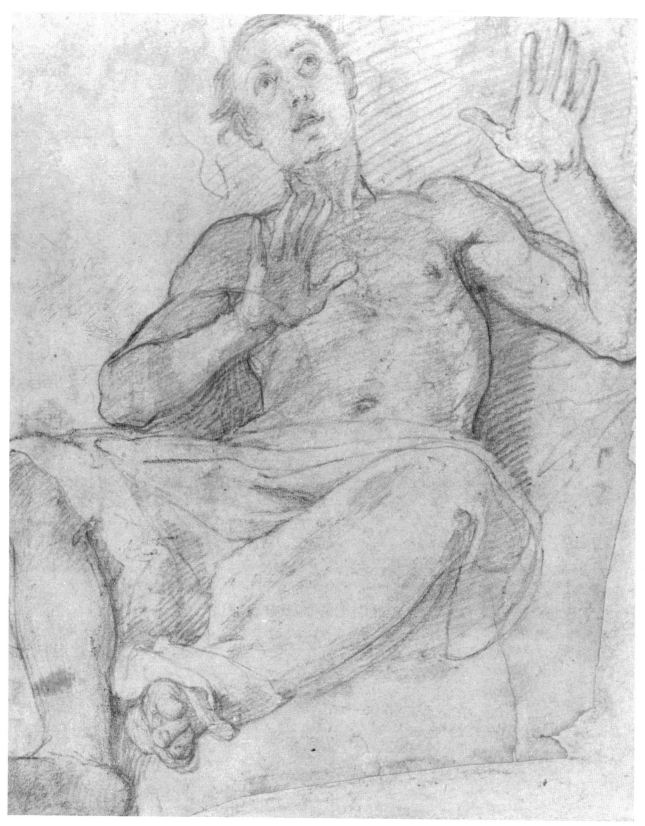

58

fig. 27, Federico Zuccaro,
Christ Raising the Son of the Widow of Nain,
Museo dell'Opera del Duomo, Orvieto

fig. 28, Jacob Matham after Federico Zuccaro,
Christ Raising the Son of the Widow of Nain,
The Metropolitan Museum of Art,
The Elisha Whittelsey Collection,
The Elisha Whittelsey Fund, 1951

FEDERICO ZUCCARO

59 *Head of an Old Man with a Beard* c. 1568

Red and black chalk
114 x 76 mm. (4 ½ x 3 inches)
The Snite Museum of Art, University of Notre Dame, on extended loan as a
promised gift from Mr. John D. Reilly, L85.45.30

PROVENANCE: John Minor Wisdom, New Orleans

LITERATURE: none

EXHIBITIONS: Spiro and Coleman 1987, no. 24, repr.

This drawing is of a common type associated with Federico. A disproportionate number of portraits in red and black chalk have, at one time or another, been attributed to the artist. This one seems consistent in stylistic terms with his work in chalk at the time of his commission to paint for the Orvieto cathedral in the late 1560's. This portrait head is similar to one that appeared on the London market some years ago (see *The Burlington Magazine*, 120, December, 1978, p.xliv).

This sketch, probably cut from a larger sheet of studies, bears a general resemblance to the bystanders in both of Federico's works for the Orvieto project, *The Healing of the Blind Man* and the *Raising of the Child of the Widow of Nain* (cat. no. 58).

59

FEDERICO ZUCCARO

60 *Coronation of the Virgin* c. 1570

Inscribed in ink in 17th century hand lower center: *Frederico Zucchero* and *1570-d*
Pen and ink with brown wash heightened with white over traces of black chalk
573 x 427 mm. (22 ½ x 16 ¾ inches) overall measurement including enframing devices by the artist.
Private Collection

PROVENANCE: Nicholas Lanier, London (Lugt 2885); Nicolaes Flinck, Rotterdam (Lugt 959); The Dukes of Devonshire, Chatsworth, no.199; sale, Christie's, London 3 July 1984 lot 45.

LITERATURE: Gere 1966a, p.341.

EXHIBITIONS: Byam Shaw 1969/73, no.74; Aarhus 1973, no.44.

When Taddeo Zuccaro died in 1566, among the various commissions left at some point of completion was the high altarpiece for the Roman church of S. Lorenzo in Damaso. While the sources, specifically Vasari and Federico's notations in the margins of his copy of the 1568 edition of the *Vite*, present some degree of ambiguity as to how far Taddeo was able to proceed with the commission, it seems probable that the final version of the painting, for which the present drawing served as the *modello*, exists as something of a compromise of Federico's making, combining a lower half that remains fairly true to his brother's idea with an upper tier that represents a late change of Federico's invention.

Surviving drawings in the Uffizi and the Ashmolean by Taddeo suggest that he had in mind a painting based on the model of Raphael's *Madonna of Foligno* where a vision of the Virgin and Child appears in the sky between pairs of saints. Included in the background was to have been the martyrdom of Saint Lawrence on the gridiron (cf. the study by Taddeo in the Ashmolean, Oxford, see Gere 1969a, pl. 173). Federico combined these elements in the drawing now in the Metropolitan Museum (cat. no. 61). At a late date, Federico introduced the motif of the *Coronation of the Virgin* in the upper half, designed the ornamental enframing elements and prepared a copy (now in Bremen's Kunsthalle, 1031, ill. in Bierens de Haan 1948, fig.41) for Cornelis Cort to be used as the model for his

Federico Vaccharo

60

engraving (fig. 29). The figure of the Virgin might have well been taken from the *verso* of the drawing in the Ferretti Collection, the *recto* of which carries the group of Apostles for the Pucci Chapel, another commission left incomplete by Taddeo (cat. no. 45).

fig. 29, C. Cort after Federico Zuccaro, *Coronation of the Virgin with Saints Sixtus and Lawrence,* The Metropolitan Museum of Art, New York, The Elisha Whittelsey Collection, The Elisha Whittelsey Fund, 1951

The ex-Chatsworth drawing is arguably the most important drawing by Federico in North America. Beneath the Coronation are Saints Paul and Lawrence on the left and Damasus and Peter on the right. The martyrdom itself, seen in the middleground, is reminiscent of Titian's altarpiece in the church of the Gesuiti, Venice, a work certainly remembered by Federico from his first journey there in 1564-5. The frame capitals are decorated with fleur-de-lis, the device of the Farnese, the commissioners of the work. In the lower corners are the artist's own *stèmmi*, the sugar cones with lilies.

The exact date of the completion of the altarpiece and the late *modelli* for it is difficult to determine. In the 1568 edition of Vasari the altarpiece is still referred to as unfinished. The Cort engraving is dated 1576. Thus, the inscription *1570-d* on the drawing makes sense as a possible date.

In addition to the drawings mentioned, a related sketch of the two angels on either side of the Coronation is in the Kupferstichkabinett, Cologne (1399a/b). Another related drawing is in the Albertina (Stix and Fröhlich-Bum 1932, no. 745). A third drawing of an angel possibly related to the commission is on the German art market (cf. sale, Christie's London, 4 July 1989, lot 47).

EXHIBITED IN MILWAUKEE ONLY

FEDERICO ZUCCARO

61 *The Virgin and Child Appearing to Saints Peter, Damasus, Lawrence and Paul; the Martyrdom of Saint Lawrence in the Background* c. 1568

Inscribed or signed on strip affixed to lower right: *Federicus Zuccarus 1585* or *1568* (?)
Pen and ink with pale brown wash over traces of red and black chalk.
367 x 244 mm. (14 ⁷⁄₁₆ x 9 ⁹⁄₁₆ inches)
Metropolitan Museum of Art, New York, Gift of John Steiner, 1977.76

PROVENANCE: Pierre Crozat, Paris (Lugt 2951); Sir Charles Greville (Lugt 549); Earl of Warwick (Lugt 2600); sale, Christie's, London 20-21 May 1896, part of lot 453; Mrs. D. Appleton, London; sale, Sotheby's, London 9 July 1973, lot 68; John Steiner, Larchmont, New York.

LITERATURE: Gere 1966a, pp.341-343; Gere 1969a, p.127; Bean 1982, no.275.

EXHIBITIONS: none

This drawing is an early overall compositional solution by Federico for the S. Lorenzo in Damaso altarpiece (fig. 29), executed using the preliminary sketches left behind by Taddeo at his death. The general organization was inspired by Raphael's *Madonna of Foligno*. In the final design, Federico would replace the Virgin and Child with a grander *Coronation of the Virgin,* abandon Taddeo's original pose for Saint Lawrence on the gridiron and reverse the arrangement of the foreground saints, placing Peter and Damasus on the right and Paul and Lawrence on the left.

A variant of the scene of the *Martyrdom of Saint Lawrence* is to be found in the central panel for the high altarpiece executed by Federico around 1587 in the Escorial.

Federicus Zuccarus 1605

61

FEDERICO ZUCCARO

62 *Angels and Putti in the Clouds* 1565-71

Red and black chalk over graphite(?) incised with stylus, squared with red chalk
397 x 272 mm. (15 ⅝ x 10 ¾ inches)
National Gallery of Art, Washington, D.C. Ailsa Mellon Bruce Fund, 1971.23.1

PROVENANCE: Charles Mewes (mark not in Lugt); Nathan Chaiken

LITERATURE: Washington 1974, p. 55, no. 18.

EXHIBITIONS: Olszewski 1981, no. 76, repr. p. 102.

The year 1566 was a momentous one for Federico Zuccaro. In addition to the death of his brother which left him a number of projects to be finished including the decorations at the Palazzo Farnese, Villa Farnese and Pucci Chapel, Federico was independently at work on an easel painting for the Duke of Urbino, working at the Villa d'Este, Tivoli and on frescoes in the Sala Regia at the Vatican. He also was painting a large fresco of *The Annunciation with Prophets who Preached the Coming of the Messiah* for the church of S. Maria Annunziata in Rome. This edifice was destroyed in 1626 to make room for the church of S. Ignazio. Before it was destroyed the painting was reproduced in a large engraving in two sheets by Cornelis Cort (overall measurement 465 x 694 mm.) executed in 1571 (fig. 30; see Bierens de Haan, 1948, no. 26 for related works).

fig. 30, Cornelis Cort after Federico Zuccaro, *Annunciation with Prophets*, 1571, The Harvard University Art Museums,
Gift of Belinda L. Randall from the John Witt Randall Collection

62

In this composition, in a semicircular configuration, the Annunciation takes places between six prophets and beneath God the Father surrounded by angels. The National Gallery drawing refers to the right hand group of angels. It is very close, but not identical in either size or content, to one of two drawings representing the upper section of the composition, previously in the Rosenbach and British Rail collections and presently on the art market (fig. 31, see Gere 1970, p.128, no. 10). There are also stylistic differences that suggest, while both drawings might be by Federico, one drawing could be a related study for the fresco and date to 1566 and the other might be a drawing for the print and, thus, date five years later. Because the Washington drawing is both incised and squared with a very small gridwork, it is intriguing to speculate that it served the function of a model for part of the Cort engraving. On occasion, Federico would send designs to Cort and others to be engraved.

Related drawings for this commission are in the Uffizi (818 S.); Louvre (4539, Gere 1969b, no. 51); National Gallery of Scotland, Edinburgh (D 2900, see Andrews 1968, fig. 884 as follower), Gijon (Instituto Jovellanos, destroyed) and two sketches recently on the art market (see *Master Drawings* 3-20 May, 1989, Colnaghi, New York, nos. 2 and 3).

fig. 31, Federico Zuccaro,
Angels on Clouds,
New York, art market

FEDERICO ZUCCARO

63   *Design for a Basemento: Saint Catherine in Prison
Converting the Empress Faustina* c. 1570-73

Signed in cartouche lower center: *Federicus Zuccarus/Annorum Trex
Decimi/Corscnae*
Inscribed upper right in ink: *ch.*
Pen and ink with brown wash, heightened with white over red chalk, on
faded blue paper.
290 x 407 mm. (10 ½ x 15 ¾ inches)
Mr. and Mrs. David Tobey, New York

PROVENANCE: Michel Gaud; sale, Sotheby's Monaco, 20 June 1987, no. 106.

LITERATURE: none

EXHIBITIONS: none

Recently cleaned and restored, this drawing is a welcome addition to
Federico's *oeuvre*. It is one of several studies for the scene in prison where
Catherine of Alexandria converts the Empress Faustina to Christianity. It
was originally intended as a decoration for the basement wall of the choir of S.
Caterina dei Funari in Rome. In its final form, the scene was included as an
overdoor decoration (fig. 32). On either side of the narrative scene are simulated
sculptures of Saints Saturninus and Simon, each flanked by figures holding the
saints' attributes.

fig. 32, Federico Zuccaro, *St. Catherine in Prison*, S. Caterina dei Funari, Rome

This is an important drawing for several reasons. First and foremost, because it is one of the infrequent drawings signed by the artist in his preferred Latinized spelling *Federicus Zuccarus* in the cartouche. Since it also carries the inscription *Annorum Trex Decimi* ("in his thirtieth year"), the drawing should be an important document in dating Federico's decorations for S. Caterina dei Funari. However, Federico's date of birth still remains uncertain. In favor of a birth date of 1543, we have his *Il Passaggio* of 1606 where he refers to himself as sixty-three years old (Körte 1935, p. 70), and Baglione (1733, p. 118) reports that he died in 1609 at the age of sixty-six. Opposing evidence suggesting a birth date of 1540 or 1541 is a landscape drawing with hunters in the Uffizi inscribed *FEDERICUS/ Z CCARUS. FA. AS. MDLXV/ ETATS. SVE. XXV*, thereby making him twenty-five in 1565. Further complicating the issue is the signed fresco of the *Disrobing of Christ* for the Church of S. Rocco in Parma that indicates the artist was sixty-nine years old in 1608. Logic would dictate that the memory and motivation of a twenty-five year old would be more trustworthy in reporting his age than a person at the end of his life. While the uncertainty has not been entirely resolved, it does seem likely that, if one accepts the birth date for Federico of 1540-41, the drawings for S. Caterina dei Funari were executed in 1570-71.

The Tobey drawing is also important because it was virtually unknown until the summer of 1987. Two other drawings for this theme exist, one, almost identical though smaller and minus the lowest section with the cartouche, once in the Rosenbach/British Rail collections and now on the art market (fig. 33) and the other, minus the architectural setting and simulated sculptural saints in the Rijksprentenkabinet (1981.37, see Frerichs 1981, no. 164). The Amsterdam drawing is much closer to the finished painting. In all three drawings Federico utilized the visual *concetto* of a view through prison bars into Catherine's cell, a motif that ultimately was abandoned in the S. Caterina dei Funari frescoes, but utilized later in his lunette of *Saint Peter Freed from Prison* in the Pauline Chapel of 1580.

fig. 33, Federico Zuccaro, *St. Catherine in Prison*, New York, art market

FEDERICO ZUCCARO

64 *Disputation of Saint Catherine of Alexandria* 1570-1573

Inscribed lower center in ink by later hand: *Fred. Zucchero*
Pen and ink with brown wash over graphite, heightened with white,
squared in graphite
334 x 423 mm. (13 x 16 ⅞ inches)
National Gallery of Art, Washington, D.C., Ailsa Mellon Bruce Fund
1981.89.1

PROVENANCE: Earl of Pembroke, Wilton House; H. Shickman, New
York; David Rust, Washington, D.C.

LITERATURE: Gere 1969b, p.60; Pouncey and Gere 1983, pp. 190-91.

EXHIBITIONS: *Exhibition of Old Master Drawings at the H. Shickman
Gallery*, New York, 1968, no. 14.

This is one of three extensive compositional studies for one of the frescoes in the church of S. Caterina dei Funari, Rome (fig. 34). The other two drawings are in the Louvre (4449 and 4450) and the National Gallery sketch is thought to fall, when the drawings are placed in sequence, between Louvre 4449 and 4450. In the British Museum (1966-12-10-4) there is a rather quick sketch for the right half of the composition which represents the very first idea for the project. One of the major areas of change among the various studies centers on the architectural background elements that range from triumphal arches and obelisks to circularly planned temples and massive palaces. Also, the sculpture of a soldier on the right changes from being shown holding a sword to holding a lance and shield. Also, the group in the lower left corner, undergoes changes between the National Gallery drawing and the final painting.

fig. 34, Federico Zuccaro,
Disputation of St. Catherine,
S. Caterina dei Funari

The scene portrays Catherine of Alexandria defending the faith before the tyrant Maxentius. To the right associates of Maxentius, converted by Catherine's words, are martyred. The other frescoes in the cycle are *Catherine Converting the Empress Faustina* (also represented by a drawing in this exhibition, cat. no. 63) and the *Martyrdom of Saint Catherine.*

The church itself was completed in 1564 and it is assumed, but not proven, that Federico's paintings were executed in the years 1572-73 (see Gere 1969b, p. 60 and Körte 1935, p.73). There is circumstantial evidence, however, that the drawings for this commission were executed in 1570-71 (see preceding entry).

Other related drawings are found in the Ashmolean, Oxford (Parker, II, no. 751); Kupferstichkabinett, Berlin (2nd Garnitur, 22503); the Uffizi (11038 and 1103); and an oil sketch on paper for the lower left hand group in the British Museum (ff. 1-27).

FEDERICO ZUCCARO

65 *A Seated Sibyl* 1573
verso: *Study of an Arm*

Black chalk on blue paper
268 x 175 mm. (10 ⅝ x 6 ⅞ inches)
The Saint Louis Art Museum, Mary Powell Tribute Fund 74.1970

PROVENANCE: Sale Sotheby's, London, 9 April, 1970, lot 11; P. & D. Colnaghi, London.

LITERATURE: "Drawings by Federico Zuccaro and Sir Edward John Poynter," *City Art Museum of Saint Louis: Bulletin*, n.s. VI, no. 4, 1970, pp. 4-7, repr. p. 5.

EXHIBITIONS: *Old Master Drawings*, P. & D. Colnaghi, London, 1970, no. 3; Neilson, 1972, no. 14.

This drawing is a study for the sibyl in the upper left hand portion of the frescoed entry wall of the Oratorio del Gonfalone, Rome (fig. 35). The sibyl and prophet on this section of the wall are placed above the scene of the *Flagellation* also by Federico which carries the date 1573. The other paintings in the oratory, representing moments in the Passion of Christ, were executed by Federico's contemporaries Jacopo Bertoia, Livio Agresti, Cesare Nebbia, Raffaellino da Reggio and Matteo da Lecce in a complex interweaving of simulated architectural elements, sculptures and *quadri riportati* in much the same manner as the Sala dei Fasti Farnesiani (see *Oltre Raffaello: aspetti della cultura figurativa del cinquecento romano*, Rome, 1984, pp. 145-161).

The tablets held by the angel behind the prophet reads *ET/FVI FLA/GELLATO/TOTA DIE* and on the knee of the sibyl *ET/ CASTIGA/TIO MEA/IN/MATV/TINIS.* Read together they comprise the fourteenth verse of the 73rd Psalm ("For all the day long have I been plagued and chastened every morning."), certainly an appropriated reference to the chastisement of Christ that is taking place below.

Related drawings to this project are in the Louvre (4404); Albertina (609); Ratjen Foundation, Vaduz; Royal Library, Turin (15 869); Nationalmuseum, Stockholm (863/478) and Princeton University Art Museum (59-29, a copy). Unlike the Saint Louis sketch, these other drawings represent the entire scene. The present drawing is also the only drawing executed in chalk rather than ink.

fig. 35, Federico Zuccaro, *Prophet and Sibyl*, Oratorio del Gonfalone, Rome

DRAWINGS FOR THE CUPOLA,
S. MARIA DEI FIORE, FLORENCE 66-71

In November,1575, Federico Zuccaro went to Florence to complete the work of decorating the inside of the cupola of the cathedral of S. Maria dei Fiore started by Giorgio Vasari in 1572 and left unfinished at his death in 1574. At that point only the uppermost zone of the frescoes were finished. The actual painting of Federico's portion of the frescoes began in August, 1576. They were unveiled on August 19, 1579 (fig. 36).

In keeping with contemporary practice, a written program for the imagery of the cupola had been developed for Vasari by the erudite Florentine humanist Vincenzo Borghini, prior of the Foundling Hospital. Borghini's program for a *Last Judgment* was based on Dante's *Divine Comedy* and was followed by Federico who used compositional drawings by Vasari as his point of departure.

In the Bibliotheca Hertziana, Rome is a painting by Federico of himself discussing the decoration of the cupola with Borghini (Heikamp 1967, fig. 13b).

Several kinds of drawings survive for this project. The first are the large segments of the eight inner faces of the cupola. Such drawings are probably those mentioned in Federico's inventory (Körte 1935, p.83). Others are quick pen sketches for narrative vignettes, usually studies for the saved or damned souls. The third are the chalk studies made from life in Vallombrosa and elsewhere in and around Florence which would serve as models for the depictions of saints, kings and even family members arranged in the third tier from the bottom.

Zuccaro would later execute an abbreviated version of the Duomo's decorations in the vault of the Capella S. Giacinto in the Roman church of S. Sabina in 1600 (fig. 37).

NORTH

NORTHWEST

NORTHEAST

WEST

EAST

SOUTHWEST

SOUTHEAST

SOUTH

fig. 36, Federico Zuccaro, *Last Judgment*, Cupola, S. Maria dei Fiore, Florence

fig. 37, Federico Zuccaro, *The Glorification of St. Hyacinth*, S. Sabina, Rome

FEDERICO ZUCCARO

66 *Study for a Scene from the Last Judgment* c. 1576-79

Pen and ink with brown wash over red chalk
448 x 243 mm. (17 ⅝ x 9 ½ inches)
Metropolitan Museum of Art, New York, Rogers Fund, 1961, 61.53

PROVENANCE: Jacques Seligmann and Co., New York; purchased 1961

LITERATURE: "Notable Works now on the Market," *The Burlington Magazine,* June 1960, pl. VI; Frerichs 1981, p. 93 under no. 382; Bean 1982, no. 277; Gere and Pouncey 1983, I, p. 196 under no. 309.

EXHIBITIONS: none

This drawing is a preliminary study for the west octant of the cupola. It is entirely by Federico's own hand, some of the pen lines having been reinforced. While the general scheme of this section was maintained in the fresco, a number of small changes in pose and activity of the figures were effected between this stage and the final version, such as reducing the number of figures in the background vignette, altering the poses of the trumpeting angels and the gesture of the winged virtue in the center. Federico also eliminated the figures of ecclesiastical power from the upper zone and replaced them with more crowned heads of state (cf. cat. no. 67).

The figures read from top to bottom: one of the elders of the Apocalypse, angels carrying the crown of thorns, representatives of secular and ecclesiastical power, allegorical figures of Mercy flanked by Good Council and Justice, and the avaricious punished in Hell, some being beaten or choked with money bags.

While there are many extant drawings for the various zones of the Duomo project, one like this is very rare because of its early overall state of conception, executed before smaller sections of each octant became absolutely determined. A number of these more specific drawings were probably executed by Federico's assistants.

Drawings related to this section of the cupola are in Amsterdam (Rijksprentenkabinet A 2189), London (British Museum 1862-10-11-189 and 1953-7-31-48) and the Fogg Art Museum at Harvard University (cat. no. 67).

FEDERICO ZUCCARO

67 *Study for the West Octant of the*
Cupola of the Florentine Cathedral c. 1576-79

Pen and ink with brown wash with local additions of yellow-brown wash.
544 x 414 mm. (21 ½ x 16 ⅜ inches)
Fogg Art Museum, Harvard University, Cambridge, Massachusetts Gift of
Sabatino Abate, Jr., in honor of Professor Konrad Oberhuber 1987.3

PROVENANCE: W. Apolloni, Rome; William Schab, New York; Sabatino
Abate, Jr., Boston

LITERATURE: Gere and Pouncey 1983, I, p. 195 under no. 308.

EXHIBITIONS: Apolloni 1978, no. 10, pl.V.

Portraying the upper three zones of the west octant of the interior of the Duomo cupola decorations, this drawing is a more advanced rendering of the upper half of the section sketched out in the Metropolitan Museum's sheet (see preceding entry). In regard to content, one of the changes made at this juncture was the removal of the figures of ecclesiastical power and their replacement with more characterizations of kings and emperors. A second change was the adjustment of Mercy's attributes (cf. cat. no. 66). In the Metropolitan Museum's drawing she holds a book with an "alpha" on it in her left hand and distributes what appear to be flowers or alms with her other hand. In the Fogg's drawing the book is removed and she spreads her mantle and protects several representatives of humanity with it. In the final fresco, she is shown in the more traditional *misericordia* pose with both arms spreading her mantle.

In stylistic terms, the two drawings diverge in somewhat the same manner as found in the various studies for *The Submission of Emperor Frederick Barbarossa* (cat. nos. 86-89). As the composition became more established and the drawings larger, Federico tended to concentrate more on the use of wash to draw out the volumes more fully. This is particularly true of the modeling of the faces. In the upper portion of the Fogg drawing, the multitude of background angels and cherubim are drawn in broad, and somewhat pedestrian, outlines, a detail that might indicate the beginning of studio participation at this point in the process.

FEDERICO ZUCCARO

68 *Study for the Southwest Octant of the Cupola of the Florentine Cathedral* c. 1576-79

Pen and ink with brown wash
419 x 555 mm. (16 ½ x 21 ⅝ inches)
Courtesy Hill-Stone Inc., New York

PROVENANCE: W. Appoloni, Rome; Sabatino Abate, Jr., Boston

LITERATURE: Gere and Pouncey 1983, I, p. 195, under no. 308.

EXHIBITIONS: Apolloni 1978, no. 9, pl.IV

Because of their almost identical sheet sizes, their similar states of preservation, and their presumed history in the same collections until the last decade, this drawing is likely a mate of the preceding work at the Fogg Art Museum. It represents the central zones of the southwest octant of Federico's frescoes for the Duomo in Florence. In this section are represented, according to Vincenzo Borghini's program, the "rest of Christendom...martyrs, widows, poor, rich, the leisured, the workers...." As Heikamp (1967, p.50 ff.) has noted, this was also the area where the artist chose to portray a number of family members and associates on the Duomo commission including himself, Taddeo, Giorgio Vasari, Giambologna and Don Benedetto Borghini, although these characterizations do not take specific form in the Hill-Stone drawing. Other figures, including family members such as Ottaviano and Antonia Zuccaro, the artist's parents, do appear in the left hand group. A number of portrait studies were utilized for this purpose. Among the surviving examples are the studies for Abbot Niccolò Ungaro (Stockholm, Nationalmuseum, 494), Don Benedetto Borghini (Paris, Ecole des Beaux-Arts 443v.) and Antonia Zuccaro (Chatsworth 734).

Below the zone portraying the friends and family of Federico Zuccaro is the allegorical personification of the beatitude "Blessed are the Poor in Spirit" flanked by "The Fear of God" on the left and Humility on the right. These figures were transferred to the cupola without changes.

A repetition of the Hill-Stone drawing is in the British Museum and included in their catalogue as "probably by Federico himself." I think, however, that the more perfunctory execution of many details makes it a candidate for workshop attribution.

One last aspect of the large scale Duomo drawings needs to be considered. We know that full sheets and portions of sheets existed in several versions. The purpose of these versions has been logically assumed to represent copies made in the workshop and then possibly distributed to the other artists responsible for executing the project. One use has not hitherto been suggested. In the Bibliotheca Hertziana in Rome is a painting on panel of Vincenzo Borghini conversing with Federico Zuccaro before a sectioned model of the cathedral's cupola. Standing about two and a half or three feet high, the interior of the model is decorated with designs for the fresco project on what appears to be paper applied to the inside. Is it possible that some of these drawings of the eight sections were designed to be used in this manner? This might account for the sizes of fragments such as this one and the drawing at Harvard.

FEDERICO ZUCCARO

69 *Study for the Saved in the Last Judgment* c. 1576-79

Pen and ink with brown wash; squared in red chalk
115 x 158 mm. (4 ½ x 6 ¼ inches)
The Art Institute of Chicago, Leonora Hall Gurley Memorial Collection
1922.2846

PROVENANCE: Frederick R. Aikman (sold March 14, 1913); William F.E. Gurley (mark not in Lugt)

LITERATURE: Middeldorf 1929, pp.11-14, fig.3; Heikamp 1967, p.63, n.19

EXHIBITIONS: none

This is one of the fluid and quick sketches that Federico created for the lower zone of the Duomo frescoes. It is a study for the background scene on the northwest octant of the sequence. Two other studies from this portion of the decorations have turned up on the London art market quite recently (figs. 38 and 39).

69

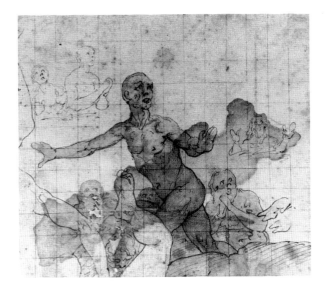

fig. 38, Federico Zuccaro,
Study for the Florentine Duomo, art market

fig. 39, Federico Zuccaro,
Study for the Florentine Duomo, art market

FEDERICO ZUCCARO

70 *Two Putti* c. 1576-79

Pen and ink with brown wash over red chalk. Watermark: eagle in a circle
(cf. Briquet 208) Pisa 1575-79
225 x 133 mm. (8 ⅞ x 5 ¼ inches)
National Gallery of Canada, Ottawa 55 77 0. 149

PROVENANCE: Lionel Lucas, London (Lugt supp. 1733a); sale, Christie's
London 9 Dec. 1949; Acquired from P. & D. Colnaghi, London, 1950.

LITERATURE: Popham and Fenwick 1965, no. 43 repr; Vitzthum 1965,
p.409; Heikamp 1967, p.63, n.19; Smith 1978, p.29ff, fig.8.

EXHIBITIONS: none

Walter Vitzthum first identified this drawing as a study for two of the putti supporting the architecture below the lantern of the Florentine cathedral of S. Maria dei Fiore. The upper cherub is the one actually used in the painting of the upper zone of the northwest octant, for which the Chicago sketch was also destined (see previous entry).

The *pentimenti* on this sheet indicate Federico's quick working method and the adjustments that were made along the way on even the smallest details for the Duomo project.

These two putti also appear in larger studies in the Uffizi (1100F), the art museum of the University of Michigan (1973/2.81) and the British Museum (1863-5-9-63).

70

FEDERICO ZUCCARO

71 *Saint Romuald* c. 1576-79

Inscribed by the artist on verso in chalk: *il padre fra Stefano porcuratori dell'*
ordine Abita de romito di Camaldoti; on recto upper left in ink: *20*
Black and red chalks. Watermark: fleur-de-lis inscribed within a circle
(Briquet 7318), Pisa 1581-84
267 x 160 mm (10 ½ x 6 ⁵⁄₁₆ inches)
Woodner Family Collection, New York WD-860

PROVENANCE: unknown

LITERATURE: none

EXHIBITIONS: none

This drawing is certainly a study for the figure of Saint Romuald for the
south octant of the cupola decorations, dedicated to poverty and humility,
for the Florentine Cathedral. The identity is confirmed by the inscription
on the *verso* identifying the subject as "Brother Stephen, procurator of the order
dressed as a Camaldolese hermit." Saint Romuald (c.950-1027) was the founder
of the Camaldolites, a small independent order of Benedictines located near
Arezzo. The Camaldolites dressed in white as the figure is portrayed in the
fresco. Interestingly, Romuald was not canonized until 1595 so his appearance
among the hermit saints and martyrs in Federico's fresco might represent the
strength of his following as his sainthood was being considered by the Church.
The figure is holding a model of a church, typically a symbol of the saint, and
also a rosary, normally a symbol of Saint Benedict.

Most of Federico's sketching of monastics at this point took place while he was
visiting the hermitage church of Badia di Vallombrosa in August of 1576 and
1577. It is quite probable, again owing to the inscription that resembles several
others done at this time, that he sketched Brother Stephen at this time and found
the opportunity of including him among the figures on the cupola as he did, for
example, with the Abbot of Vallombrosa, Niccolò Ungaro who is located below
and to the left of Saint Romuald. The preparatory inscribed sketch in black and
red chalks is in the Nationalmuseum in Stockholm (494).

It seems that Federico might have worked out his overall compositional idea
first for a section of the frescoes. He, then, would make individual studies based
on his preconceived set of poses after which, small adjustments of pose or
gestures would be incorporated into a final *modello* or the fresco itself.

71

A copy of the Woodner sketch with the saint wearing a longer beard is in the Louvre (4558). It is possible that this figure was used later by Federico, in reverse, on the vault of the chapel of Saint Hyacinth in S. Sabina, Rome, executed toward the end of his life in 1600 (fig. 37).

FEDERICO ZUCCARO

72 *Portrait of a Man* c. 1576-79
verso: *Fragment of a Figure*

Black and red chalk
149 x 112 mm. (5 ⅞ x 4 ⅜ inches)
Fogg Art Museum, Harvard University, Cambridge, Massachusetts The
Marion H. Phinney Fund 1964.139

PROVENANCE: Yvonne Ffrench, London; acquired in 1964

LITERATURE: none

EXHIBITIONS: *Old Master Drawings, Y. Ffrench*, London, Alpine Club,
10-21 November, 1964, no.3, repr.; Tokyo 1979, no.23, repr.

The cataloguer of the Tokyo exhibition has expressed the opinion, echoing that of Detlef Heikamp, that this drawing is a portrait sketch from the late period of Federico's work. This may be attributable to the finer and softer modeling of the chalks which stands apart somewhat from the many red and black chalk studies made by the artist during his Florentine sojourn, many of which were included in decorations for the Duomo. While this might be the case,

72 *verso*

72 *recto*

it should be noted that the figure bears a close resemblance to that of Saint Anthony of Padua on the south octant of the cupola decorations.

The drawing is a typical and very fine example of Federico's portrait style at this very productive point in his career.

FEDERICO ZUCCARO

73 *Half-Length Portrait of a Bearded Old Man* c. 1576-79

Black and red chalk
270 x 303 mm. (10 $^{11}/_{16}$ x 12 inches)
The Rosenbach Museum and Library, Philadelphia

PROVENANCE: Benjamin West (Lugt 419); Sir Thomas Lawrence (Lugt 2445); Samuel Woodburn; Lawrence-Woodburn sale, Christie's London 4-8 June, 1860; Sir Thomas Phillipps; his daughter Mrs. Katherine Fenwick; her son T. Fitzroy Phillipps Fenwick; A.S.W. Rosenbach.

LITERATURE: Gere 1970, cat. 23, pl. 15b.

EXHIBITIONS: none

Gere has suggested that this tranquil portrait of an old man might be a study made for either the portrait of Federico's father, Ottaviano or grandfather, Taddeo for the lunettes in the Sala Terrena in the Palazzo Zuccaro, which would date the drawing to the mid-to-late 1590s. A comparison with a sketch made of Ottaviano now in Stockholm (415) lends support to the suggestion that it might represent Ottaviano, while the fact that the Rosenbach Library drawing clearly was made from life would argue against it portraying the elder Taddeo who, in the 1590s, was long dead.

Stylistically, however, the drawing is less sharply defined than most of the portrait drawings for the Palazzo Zuccaro and the possibility that this sketch belongs to the period of the Florentine Duomo decorations should not be dismissed at this point. Certainly the costume would suggest an earlier date in the sixteenth century rather than a later one.

73

FEDERICO ZUCCARO

74 *Two Men and a Young Boy Seated in a Landscape*
c. 1576-77

Inscribed in ink by contemporary hand: *questo dal N....* and in ink by a later
hand: *homme en apprendant*
Pen and ink
190 x 291 mm. (7 ½ x 11 ½ inches)
Courtesy Helen Getler Fine Art, Roslyn, New York

PROVENANCE: William H. Schab Gallery, New York.

LITERATURE: none

EXHIBITIONS: Davidson 1986, pp. 14-15.

Konrad Oberhuber was the first to attribute this drawing to Federico. The possibility that the drawing is a copy, perhaps intended as a study for print, should not be ruled out entirely. Davidson has suggested that the drawing originates from the mid-to-late 1570s when Federico was doing much *al fresco* sketching. This was also the period when one sees in Federico's art the greatest interest in recording everyday activities. Most of these drawings are in chalks and not pen and ink which might support the notion that it is a copy. However, it should also be pointed out that many of these drawings are annotated much as the fragmentary description in Italian demonstrates in this case. Also, similar figures are found, for example, in the middleground of a chalk sketch in the Louvre (4582, ill. in Heikamp 1967, pl 31).

A number of genre activities were woven into the context of the decoration of the Casa Zuccaro in Florence where Federico labored when not working on the Duomo cupola frescoes in the years 1577-79. The pursuit and enjoyment of the literary and fine arts in a relaxed natural setting was appropriate fodder for these decorations. It is also likely that the artist was made more receptive to this manner of subject through his exposure to Venetian painting, particularly that of Giorgione and Titian, during his first Venetian sojourn during 1563-65.

FEDERICO ZUCCARO

75 *Half-Length Figure of a Bearded Man Reading a Book* c. 1575-79

Inscribed upper right in ink: a collector's paraphe(?) and a numeral
Black and red chalks
120 x 85 mm. (4 ¾ x 3 ⁷⁄₁₆ inches)
Dr. Carlo M. Croce, Philadelphia

PROVENANCE: Sale, Christie's New York, 14 January 1986 lot 244.

LITERATURE: none

EXHIBITIONS: none

Certainly one of the many quick chalk sketches made by Federico while in Florence in the last half of the 1570's, this drawing belongs to that group of genre studies that seems to prefigure similar work by the Carracci.

75

FEDERICO ZUCCARO

76   *Head and Shoulders of a Woman* c. 1575-79

Black and red chalk
126 x 96 mm (5 x 3 ¾ inches)
Museum of Fine Arts, Boston, Gift of Henry P. Rossiter, 1952.1762

PROVENANCE: J. Richardson, Jr. (Lugt 2178); Sir Joshua Reynolds (Lugt 2364); H.F. Sewall.

LITERATURE: Macandrew 1983, p. 30, no. 24.

EXHIBITIONS: none

Federico Zuccaro popularized the technique of executing portrait or genre studies in black and red chalk, in fact so much so that scores of drawings have been attributed to him on the basis of their medium alone. Much material of lesser quality has, therefore, diluted the overall impression of Federico's talents as an artist with the critical public.

The fact that this drawing is not particularly prepossessing at first glance is perhaps owing more to its rather plain subject and the strong, almost harsh use of light. It is, however, one of the more psychologically intense of Federico's portrait sketches and rates high in a qualitative sense. It belongs to the period of his greatest interests in this form of representation, when he was actively engaged in Florence on the frescoes for the cupola of the Duomo, 1575-79.

76

FEDERICO ZUCCARO

77 *Lady Putting on her Stockings* c. 1575-82
verso: *A Female Figure Alighting from a Chariot*

Graphite and red chalk
162 x 145 mm. (6 ⅜ x 5 ¾ inches)
The Nelson-Atkins Museum of Art, Kansas City, Gift of Mr. Milton
McGreevy to the Nelson Gallery Foundation F61-55/7

PROVENANCE: unknown

LITERATURE: none

EXHIBITIONS: none

This drawing is typical of Federico's numerous genre studies in chalk made during his time in Florence from 1575-79 (see Heikamp 1967). While a number of these drawings were included in the decoration of the Florentine Duomo, some were utilized at later moments in his career, for example in the *Submission of Emperor Frederick Barbarossa to Pope Alexander III* of 1582 in Venice (cat. nos. 86-88). While the Kansas City drawing does not appear to have been specifically incorporated into an existing final composition, the woman does bear similarities with two drawings of a studio model who is included in the *Submission*. Shaw (1983, no.142) has suggested that the head

77 verso

77 recto

study of a woman in the Lugt Collection (1978-t.14) might be the same woman found in Christ Church's study of a kneeling woman (0216) which was used for the woman kneeling in the foreground of the *Submission*. Although not identical, the Nelson-Atkins' woman wears a similar dress and hair style that might suggest this study was made on the same day, although this is merely conjecture.

The *verso* of the drawing was recently uncovered. While suggestive of a mythological subject, such as Federico might have seen in Venice, it has not yet been identified.

FEDERICO ZUCCARO

78   *The Garden of the Liberal and Fine Arts* c. 1577-79

Inscribed on buildings from left to right: *FRVTO PESTIFERO/NON PIV SAPERE/QUOD PORTE SAPE/RE; HONORIS; VIRTUTIS; FAMAE; SPIRI/TO*
Pen and ink with brown wash, heightened with white on light brown prepared paper, squared in red chalk
225 x 368 mm. (8 ⅞ x 14 ½ inches)
The Pierpont Morgan Library, New York, The Janos Scholz Collection
1983.67

PROVENANCE: Ottaviano Zuccaro (?); William Young Ottley (possibly his sale, London, Philipe, 6-23 June 1814, lot 1489); Jonathan Richardson, Jr. (Lugt 2170); Sir Joshua Reynolds (Lugt 2364); Sir Thomas Lawrence (Lugt 2445); Samuel Woodburn (see Lugt 2584); Lawrence-Woodburn sale, London, Christie's, 4-8 June, 1860, part of lot 1074; Sir Thomas Phillipps (see Lugt 924b); his daughter, Mrs. Katherine Fenwick; her son T. Fitzroy Fenwick; A.S.W. Rosenbach, Philadelphia; John Fleming, New York; Janos Scholz, New York.

LITERATURE: Winner 1962, p. 168ff.; Paris 1965, under no. 255; Heikamp 1967, II, p.28 and pl.20; Gere 1969b, p. 63; Gere 1970, p. 129, no. 16; Van Mander 1973, fig. 5; Hermann-Fiore 1979, p. 51 repr.; Gerards-Nelissen 1983, p. 51; Ryskamp 1984, p. 317.

EXHIBITIONS: Houston 1966, no. 54; London 1968, no. 114, pl. 10; Amherst 1974, no. 79; Notre Dame 1980, no. 149.

Apollo, in the center, directs the activities of the representatives of the liberal arts (astronomy, arithmetic, music, geometry, grammar, rhetoric, and logic) and the fine arts (sculpture, painting, poetry and architecture). In the background, youths who have scaled the mountain of virtue are shown the entry to the temple of virtue and honor and connecting temple of fame. Those who make a wrong turn (to the left) encounter the dire results of not wanting to pursue knowledge.

One of Federico's many allegorical drawings of his mature period, this sketch relates, as Hermann-Fiore and others have noted, to the background of the fresco portraying *The Hero at the Crossroads*, found in the Sala Terrena in the Palazzo Zuccaro which dates to around 1593 (fig. 40). The ancient concept of the choice of the virtuous path, eventually allows the hero to ascend to the Palace of the Liberal Arts at the summit of the mountain. However, the drawing is much more elaborate than this section of the fresco and, considering that, what seems to be a proper preparatory sketch survives in Berlin (Kupferstichkabinett 25264),

fig. 40, Federico Zuccaro,
The Hero at the Crossroads,
Sala Terrena, Palazzo Zuccaro,
Bibliotheca Hertziana, Rome

it is certainly possible that the Morgan Library drawing was considered for an entirely different purpose. Heikamp (1967, II,p.28) has observed stylistic similarities between the Morgan Library drawing and one in the Louvre illustrating an *Allegory of the Vices* (23201) where a youth enters into a garden of temptations and pleasures. The correspondences extend to the sizes of the two sheets, that in the Louvre measuring (235 x 367 mm.). He suggests further that both drawings might have been destined as frescoes for the Casa Zuccaro in Florence, the decorations for which date to 1577-78, fifteen years prior to the decorations for the Roman palace. A drawing of *Summer* in the Museo Nazionale in Valetta, Malta, that does correspond to one of the frescoes in the Florentine house is, as Heikamp points out, stylistically consistent with this drawing. It is also the only one signed in Federico's hand (*Fredericus Zuccarus fecit*).

While some of the planned allegories were not to see fruition, subjects introduced into their compositions would be developed later by the artist for

238

other purposes. For example, the presence of the *Porta Virtutis* in the present Morgan Library drawing with its guardian, Minerva, would serve as the point of departure for Federico's infamous painting of the same subject in 1581 (see cat. no. 85). Also the presence of Spirito welcoming the youth as he leaves the temple of Fame presents a parallel with certain episodes from the *Life of Taddeo* of the 1590s.

In his organization and articulation of single figures, Federico draws upon the experience of Raphael's frescoes of *Parnassus* and the *School of Athens* in the Stanza della Segnatura in the Vatican.

Regarding the drawing's provenance, Bertolotti (1881, p.21), recorded in Heikamp (1967, I, p.65) mentions among the drawings left to Federico's son Ottaviano in the 1610 inventory "Un tempio della virtu". This is listed, co-incidentally, just before "Un disegno della calunnia di Bologna" a reference to one of the versions of the *Porta Virtutis*, originally designed as a response to the severe criticisms Federico experienced at the hands of the Bolognese artists (see cat. no. 85).

FEDERICO ZUCCARO

79   *Allegory of Sin* c. 1577-9

Inscribed in black chalk center and lower right by the artist:
PIANTO/PECAT(O)/SPAVENTO; lower center in ink by later hand: *Zuccaro*.
Pen and ink over black and red chalk with gray-brown wash
108 x 266 mm. (7 ½ x 10 ½ inches)
The Pierpont Morgan Library, New York, Gift of the Fellows, 1968.5

PROVENANCE: Sale, Sotheby's London 28 March 1968, lot 35.

LITERATURE: *A Review of Acquisitions 1949-1968*, The Pierpont Morgan Library, New York, 1969, p. 178.

EXHIBITIONS: none

A bearded man, dressed as a hermit sits with his hands in an attitude of prayer, flanked by a personification of weeping (*pianto*) on the left and sin, (*pecato*) as a skeleton, on the right. A figure labeled fear (*spavento*), with a lion's head, curly tail and taloned feet approaches from the right holding a torch in one hand and a scourge in the other. Before them wolves and foxes torture other animals, monsters torture small humanoid figures and lizard-like

79

monsters carouse and copulate at a table. To the right of fear, a pig wears a large grotesque human head. On the left, men dangle from a torture wheel. In the background, a castle burns.

This drawing, while typical of Federico's bent toward arcane allegory, is unusual in the high degree of Boschian imagery that is found within it. It is likely that this drawing was made at the time of the decoration of the Casa Zuccaro in Florence around 1577-79 although there is no more specific evidence to support this idea. In 1574, Federico traveled through France and the Netherlands on the way to England. While in London, Federico copied Holbein's large allegorical paintings of the *Triumph of Riches* and *The Triumph of Poverty* in the hall of the Steelyard (Berlin, Kupferstichkabinett 12886 and 12887) as well as other decidedly Northern European subjects such as *Death Attacking Two Gentlemen on Horseback* (Berlin, Kupferstichkabinett 621). This type of imagery wherein the various allegorical figures are labeled made an impression on the artist. It is likely, that he might have also come into contact with the work of Bosch or a follower at this time so that when he returned to Florence to finish his work on the *Last Judgment* and the decorations of the Casa Zuccaro, he had some of these Northern sources fresh in his mind and close at hand. By the same token, it is possible that he was impressed with the work of Bosch while at the Spanish court between 1585-88.

The identification of the subject as an allegory of sin is a serviceable one, but perhaps too simple. The mortal, cast into this landscape of devastation is threatened by fear and is comforted by sin and weeping. His faith is clearly being tempted much as in a depiction of the temptation of Saint Anthony. Perhaps this drawing is meant to convey the idea of eternal punishment for the sinful life or what fear can lead one to.

FEDERICO ZUCCARO

80 *The Liberation of Saint Peter from Prison*

Pen and ink with brown wash
242 x 203 mm. (9 ⁹⁄₁₆ x 8 inches)
Baltimore Museum of Art 1932.73.23

PROVENANCE: Robert Gilmor

LITERATURE: none

EXHIBITIONS: none

It is possible that this drawing is a first thought for, or even a rethinking of Federico's frescoed lunette in the Capella Paolina in the Vatican. After Michelangelo executed the two large frescoes in the chapel, work was interrupted until 1573 when Don Vincenzo Borghini of Florence submitted through Giorgio Vasari, a plan for the remaining decorations based on typological parallels between moments from the life of Moses and those taken from the lives of Saints Peter and Paul. The program was not acceptable to Pope Gregory XIII and the project was given to the Bolognese artist Lorenzo Sabbatini who executed three scenes (*The Stoning of Saint Stephen*, *The Curing of Paul's Blindness in the House of Ananias*, and *The Fall of Simon Magus*) before his death in 1577. Three years later, in 1580, the completion of the project was awarded to Federico Zuccaro, who painted the last fresco in December of 1581. Completion of the final details would wait until 1584, after Federico returned to Rome following his pardon (Baumgart and Biagetti 1934, pp. 57-62 and 83-93.).

The compositional device of a view through prison bars into a well lighted space was practiced already by Federico in his designs for the fresco of *Saint Catherine Converting the Empress Faustina* in the main chapel of the church of Sta. Caterina dei Funari, Rome, executed between 1570-73 (see cat. no. 63 and the sketch in the Rijksmuseum 1981:37). Zuccaro's initial inspiration for the composition might have been Raphael's *Liberation of Peter* in the Stanza of Heliodorus in the Vatican.

The largest notable difference between the Baltimore drawing and the final fresco and the only fact that argues against a connection between the two is the rectangular format of the drawing versus the semicircular one of the painting. In the other surviving sketches for the Pauline Chapel, the painted roundels for example, Federico composed his idea with the format in mind from the outset. Vasari mentions an easel painting of the subject by Federico executed in 1566 for the Duke of Urbino which might also relate to the Baltimore drawing.

Zucchero. 1529-1566.   Baltimore 1845 by R.G.

80

FEDERICO ZUCCARO

81 *The Death of Ananias*
Saint Peter Healing the Cripple

Pen and ink with brown wash
Inscribed on old mounts *Ano. Tempesti*
each 130 x 56 mm. (5 ⅛ x 2 ¼ inches)
Fogg Art Museum, Harvard University, Cambridge, Massachusetts
Acc. nos. 40.1987 and 39.1987

PROVENANCE: sale Christie's London, July 6-7, 1987, lot 117

LITERATURE: none

EXHIBITIONS: none

In spite of the inscriptions these small studies should rightly be considered the work of Federico from the early 1580's. The distinctive mitten-like hands and the open, round definition of the bearded faces are hallmarks of the artist's later and more rapid style. The subject matter and the pronounced vertically rectangular format suggest they are ideas for the remaining narrative wall frescoes in the Pauline Chapel at the Vatican.

Federico only painted one scene of the four additions to the wall decorations, *The Baptism of the Centurion*, the other three completed by Lorenzo Sabbatini (see previous catalogue no. 80). The surviving drawings for the painting (Vienna, Albertina 1135, Florence, Uffizi 11008 F. and Paris, Louvre 4442) are worked up much more completely than the Harvard sketches and since no further elaborated drawings of these particular miracles exist, it is likely that, if they were ideas for the chapel, they were discarded quite early.

81

81

FEDERICO ZUCCARO

82 *David and Goliath*
verso: *Nude Female Figure with Geese and other Studies*

Inscribed recto lower right in ink by later hand: *Zuccari* and *di Federigo Zuccaro* in ink by later hand (verso).
Pen and ink with brown wash over red chalk, the figure of Goliath lightly squared in black chalk. Verso: red chalk
304 x 252 mm. (12 x 10 inches)
Duke Roberto Ferretti, Montreal

PROVENANCE: Unidentified collector's mark; sale, Christie's London, 29 November 1983, lot 16.

LITERATURE: Krass, Katrin, *Master Drawings, 1500-1900*, London, 1987, under no. 2.

EXHIBITIONS: McTavish 1985, no. 21.

Old Testament scenes in the art of Federico Zuccaro are extremely rare except for the series of sixteen scenes from the life of Moses that he painted for the Vatican Belvedere. There is no documentary evidence that Federico ever painted David slaying Goliath. Most stylistic characteristics, especially the background figures and curious manner of defining knee caps suggest a date no later than around 1580 for this drawing.

While the figure of Goliath is squared for transfer, it seems that other parts of the drawing were used in different contexts or, at least, served as inspiration for other figures. The pose of David is very close to that of *Hercules Slaying Cacus* on the ceiling of the entrance to the Palazzo Zuccaro (see Hermann-Fiore 1979, fig. 14). On the *verso*, the red chalk allegorical figure might refer to Annibale Caro's program for the Camera dell'Aurora in the Farnese villa at Caprarola, where he suggests that in the *grotteschi* there be figures striding forth into the new day and animals such as geese and other birds that are "messengers of the day" (Vasari 1850, V, p.223).

McTavish has pointed to the possible influence of Michelangelo's spandrel group of *David Slaying Goliath* from the Sistine Chapel as a potential source of influence on Federico in this drawing. He further suggests that the Worcester drawing (see cat. no. 103) and the Ferretti sketch should be examined together. While this is true from a narrative point of view, they are stylistically very dissimilar, the Ferretti drawing being far superior in every respect.

246

82

FEDERICO ZUCCARO

83 *Rest on the Flight into Egypt* c. 1580

Inscribed on old backing: *Taddeo Zuccaro*
Pen and ink with brown wash over black chalk, squared for transfer.
469 x 377 mm. (18 ½ x 14 ⅞ inches)
Alfred Moir, Santa Barbara

PROVENANCE: Sale Sotheby's London, 3 July 1980, lot 16; sale, Sotheby's London, 23 March 1982, lot 16.

LITERATURE: none

EXHIBITIONS: Santa Barbara Art Museum, *Santa Barbara Collects Part I*, 26 Jan - 24 March 1985.

If the painting for which this drawing seems intended as a model was ever actually executed, it has not been discovered. The moment represented is the apocryphal Miracle of the Palm Tree, when the Christ Child commanded a date palm to bend so as to provide the family with sustenance during their flight. In what is perhaps a typical post-Tridentine composition, the miracle becomes a more physical reality thanks to the exertions of the angels.

The presence of the contemplative donor in the lower right corner is unusual in the work of Federico, his pose reminiscent of a figure such as that found in the *Baptism of Cornelius* in the Pauline Chapel from the 1580s, the period from which this drawing probably dates. There are other reasons to date this drawing to that decade in the artist's career, among them the poses of the acrobatic angels bending the date palm and removing some of its fruit for the Holy Family. Such angels begin to emerge in Federico's work during his painting for the cupola of the Duomo in Florence and continue to appear in subsequent late commissions, particularly the Capella degli Angeli in the Gesù and the Chapel of Saint Hyacinth in the church of S. Sabina, both in Rome. The construction and seriousness of Mary are strongly reminiscent of Michelangelo's art, for example his Vatican *Pietà*. Joseph's pose, nevertheless, stems from Raphael's art, adapting the sinuous *contrapposto* of the figure to the left of Heraclitus in the *School of Athens* in the Stanza della Segnatura (later used in the *Galatea* in the Villa Farnesina).

An earlier, and more quickly executed, study for this composition is in the Royal Library, Turin (see Bertini 1958, no. 438).

83

FEDERICO ZUCCARO

84 *The Virgin and Child with Saint Joseph, Attendant Angels, and a Group of Supplicants*

Inscribed at lower left in pen and ink *Fco. Zuccaro* and on verso, *Battista Naldini*
Pen and ink with brown wash over red chalk
293 x 230 mm. (11 ½ x 9 inches)
Metropolitan Museum of Art, New York, Rogers Fund, 1968, 68.106.2

PROVENANCE: Purchased from P. & D. Colnaghi and Co., London, 1968.

LITERATURE: Gere 1969b, p. 67 under no. 92; Byam Shaw 1976, I, pp. 156-57, under no. 547, fig. 36; Bean 1982, no. 274.

EXHIBITIONS: *Exhibition of Old Master Drawings*, P. & D. Colnaghi and Co., London, 1968, no. 10.

This drawing should be entitled *Virgin and Child with Saint Joseph, Attendant Angels and a Donor Introduced by Two Saints* and while not yet connected with any known composition by the artist, certainly represents a well thought out plan for an altarpiece. In the Louvre is a two sided drawing (12281) with the Virgin and Child with Saint Joseph on one side and a truncated and roughly sketched version of the entire composition on the *verso* (Gere 1969b, no. 92). The Christ Child differs slightly in the Louvre sketch by being represented, holding the orb of the world in his left hand, as *Salvator Mundi*. Another version of the Virgin and Child, this time seated on a cloud bank is in the collection at Christ Church, Oxford (Byam Shaw 1976, no. 547).

The dating of this drawing poses something of a problem. It should certainly be seen as dating from the same period as Louvre 11593, *The Vision of Saint Peter*, that Gere places "rather late" in the artist's career (1969b, no.100). While this is possible, a date around 1580, when he was active with decorations for the Pauline Chapel, should also be considered.

84

FEDERICO ZUCCARO

85 *Porta Virtutis* 1582?

Inscribed extensively with the names of the allegorical figures
Pen and ink with brown wash over black chalk. Watermark: Eagle in a
circle surmounted by a crown (cf. Briquet 209) Verona 1582-96.
388 x 286 mm. (15 ¼ x 11 ¼ inches)
The Pierpont Morgan Library, New York, The Janos Scholz Collection
1974.25

PROVENANCE: Norman Colville, London; purchased in London in 1949;
Janos Scholz, New York.

LITERATURE: Heikamp 1957, pp. 189-194, n.45; Heikamp 1958, p. 46ff;
Shaw 1972, pp. 57-58, no.86; Ryskamp 1984, p. 186.

EXHIBITIONS: Indianapolis 1954, no. 39, repr.; Hamburg 1963, no. 178, pl.
57; Haverkamp-Begemann and Sharp 1964, no. 54; New York 1965, I, no.
141, repr.; London 1968, no. 115; Middletown 1969, no. 14; Oberhuber and
Walker 1973, no. 10.

Subtitled *Minerva Triumphant over Ignorance and Calumny*, the painting to
which this drawing, one in Frankfurt, as well as the *modello* at Christ
Church, Oxford (fig. 41), relate landed Federico in an *imbroglio* that
resulted in his expulsion from Rome. The painting itself was executed by
Federico's student Domenico Passignano who was actually jailed for his
participation.

At times hypersensitive to criticism, Federico reacted strongly to the criticism
of the artists in Bologna in 1580 when he felt they were responsible for the
rejection by Paolo Ghiselli, the commissioner of his painting, of *The Procession
and Vision of Saint Gregory* for the church of S. Maria del Baraccano in Bologna.
His resentment took the form of a large painting, *Porta Virtutis*, that was
unveiled in Rome against the façade of the church of San Luca a Monte Santa
Maria Maggiore on 18 October 1581, the feast day of Saint Luke, the patron saint
of artists. Legal action was taken against Federico in the form of a suit for
slander and Pope Gregory XIII (Boncompagni), himself a Bolognese, banished
the artist from Rome for two years.

The general idea of the *Porta Virtutis* appeared several years earlier in the
background of Federico's drawing of the *Garden of the Liberal and Fine Arts* as a
portal of opportunity on the way to honor (cat. no. 78). In the *Porta Virtutis*,
Federico fills in this classical arch with a number of allegories. Standing in the
doorway is Minerva treading underfoot a figure of Vice. Behind her, through the

85

Portal of Virtue, one passes Study, Intelligence, the Graces and Spirito, the last two figures familiar from our knowledge of the illustrations from the *Life of Taddeo* (cat. no. 96). Cherubs representing Invention, Design, Color, and Decorum hover, holding aloft an altarpiece. In the Oxford *modello*, this painting is the same shape and in all its elements reflects the composition of the *Procession and Vision of Saint Gregory*, known from a drawing for the engraving by Aliprando Caprioli formerly in the Rosenbach and British Rail Pension Fund Collections (fig. 42) with other versions in Munich (Staatliche Graphische Sammlung 1949:29) and the Albertina (2258). What is most interesting is that in the replicas of the *Porta Virtutis* drawing that Federico sent to colleagues to defend his position, among them the Morgan Library sheet, he intentionally changed the composition in the painting above Minerva's head, obviously in an effort to disassociate the execution of this satire with the Bolognese affair. The Veronese watermark further suggests that this replica was made after Federico's banishment, perhaps while in the Veneto in 1582. It might have then been sent to a colleague.

The front of the arch is decorated with allegorical figures of Labor, Diligence, and Fame. Before the portal an artist with ass's ears, in the tradition of most portrayals of the Calumny of Apelles (see, for example the design by Federico datable to 1569, engraved by Cornelis Cort in 1572 in Hamburg, ill. in Hermann-Fiore 1979, p.49, fig. 6). Whispering in his ears are the agents of Adulation and Presumption, at his feet the beasts of Crass Ignorance and Malice. Reclined at his feet holding his leg is the personification of Envy wrapped in snakes. The three satyrs on the right, indicating Satire, Slander and Defamation gesture in frustration at the triumph of Virtue.

The complexities of the allegories did not keep Federico out of trouble and the ambiguousness of the content seemed to work as much against him as in his favor. The sketches in Frankfurt and the Morgan Library are likely those that the artist willingly sent to people interested in hearing his side of the affair. Bold and rash in its conception, reflective of a sensitivity bordering on paranoia, the *Porta Virtutis* is also an unusual visual statement and exercise in propaganda that brings the highly charged atmosphere of the Italian art world in the sixteenth century, with all its intrigues, to life.

fig. 42, Federico Zuccaro,
The Votive Procession of St. Gregory Against the Plague,
New York, art market

FEDERICO ZUCCARO

86 *The Submission of the Emperor Frederick Barbarossa to Pope Alexander III,* c. 1582

Pen and ink with brown wash over black chalk
263 x 213 mm. (10 ⅜ x 8 ⁷⁄₁₆ inches)
The Pierpont Morgan Library, New York, The Janos Scholz Collection
1973.29

PROVENANCE: Sir Thomas Lawrence (Lugt 2445); Samuel Woodburn;
Lawrence-Woodburn sale, Christie's London, 4-8 June 1860, part of lot
1074; Sir Thomas Phillipps; his daughter, Mrs. Katherine Fenwick; her son,
T. Fitzroy Phillipps Fenwick; A.S.W. Rosenbach; Janos Scholz.

LITERATURE: Gere 1970, p.132, no.21, pl.14; Scholz 1976, no.65, repr.;
Joachim and McCullagh 1979, p.40; Denison and Mules 1981, no.27; Held,
1981, p. 177; Ryskamp 1984, p.185; Goldner 1988, under no.55.

EXHIBITIONS: Venice 1957, no.25; Oakland 1959, no.82, repr.; Detroit 1960,
no. 24; Oberhuber and Walker 1973, no. 11, repr.; Los Angeles 1976, no.114,
repr.

In 1577, fire destroyed the painted decorations in the Sala del Gran Consiglio of the Doge's Palace in Venice. Among those destroyed was a painting of Emperor Frederick Barbarossa in submission kissing the foot of Pope Alexander III outside the church of San Marco. This painting was executed by Titian, completing a composition begun by Giovanni Bellini and/or Giorgione (Valconover 1960, II, p.102). In 1582, after he was banished from Rome for his affront to the Pope in composing the Porta Virtutis cartoon, Federico Zuccaro was given the task of replacing Titian's painting (not Tintoretto's, a mistake reported by Denison and Mules, corrected in Held, but repeated by Goldner). While the composition was developed at this time, the painting was not actually completed until 1603 (fig.43).

The moment celebrated is one of successful intervention by the Venetian Doge Sebastiano Ziani during the conflict between the Holy Roman Empire and the Church in 1176-77. After the capture of Barbarossa's son Otto by the Venetian fleet, the Emperor finally sued for peace and was reconciled with Pope Alexander III. Obviously, it was a moment of importance in the diplomatic history of the Venetian Republic. Titian's original design was replete with contemporary portraits of important Venetian citizens. While Federico's drawings give no indication of a similar plan, the final painting was seen as an exercise in group portraiture in an anachronistic setting.

86

As has been frequently pointed out, the Morgan Library drawing depicts a reversed viewpoint from the other surviving studies and the final painting by offering a view into the Piazza San Marco toward the Torre del Orologio rather than toward the lagoon and the Isola di S. Giorgio. The reason for this change in orientation is not entirely clear. One reason may be that the painting occupies the left half of a wall between two doors next to the scene of *Otto Sent by the Pope to his Father to Plead for Peace*, painted by Palma Il Giovane before 1587. Palma's

fig. 43, Federico Zuccaro,
The Submission of the Emperor Frederick Barbarossa to Pope Alexander III,
Venice, Ducal Palace

composition is directed toward the left and would, thus, be balanced by Federico's composition if it were directed toward the right. Such a solution might have been developed after Palma received his commission and the two artists (or their commissioner) had the opportunity to envision the results of their work.

The other notable adjustment to the composition is that in reversing the point of view, Federico also moved the activity out from under the narthex of San Marco farther into the square. In so doing he further decided to emphasize the forceful channeling of the viewer's attention to the middleground through a gauntlet of repoussoir figures, cleaving the space in a manner that the greater rectilinearity of the Morgan design does not do.

Some of the lesser details of the composition might have been inspired, at least indirectly, by Federico's experience of Salviati's fresco of the same theme in the Sala Regia at the Vatican, where both artists worked between 1563-1566. A preparatory drawing for the fresco is at the Wadsworth Atheneum (1952.409). The smiling young page looking at the viewer is another quotation from the Sala Regia, this time a self-quotation from *Emperor Henry IV Submitting to Pope Gregory VII at Canossa*, a preparatory study for which is in the Louvre (4452).

The figure leaning against the column in the lower left corner of the Morgan Library composition was later worked out with a studio model in the drawing in the Woodner Collection (cat. no. 89 *recto*)

FEDERICO ZUCCARO

87 *The Submission of the Emperor Frederick Barbarossa to Pope Alexander III* c. 1582

Black chalk, pen and ink with brown wash on two attached sheets of paper
554 x 539 mm. (21 ³⁄₁₆ x 21 ¼ inches)
The J. Paul Getty Museum, Malibu 83.GG.196

PROVENANCE: Sir Peter Lely, London (Lugt 2092); Sir William Forbes, Pitsligo; by descent, sale Christie's London, 12 April 1983, lot 10.

LITERATURE: Ward 1984, p.251; Goldner 1988, no.55, repr.

EXHIBITIONS: none

Together with the drawing in the Ian Woodner collection (cat. no. 88), this large sheet represents the final stage of the composition Federico executed for the Sala del Gran Consiglio in the Palazzo Ducale, Venice (fig. 43). The earliest surviving version of the composition is in the Pierpont Morgan Library (cat. no. 86). An intermediate design for the composition is in an English private collection (see Gere 1970, p.132, fig.1). The only major alterations in the final painting are the addition of the baldachin over the principle figures and the inclusion of what might be portraits among the retinue of both emperor and pope.

The Getty drawing is slightly larger than that in the Woodner Collection. The truncation of the left and right sides of the latter drawing and its generally deteriorated state of preservation, might indicate its use as a working drawing, while the Getty sheet seems something more approaching a drawing of record. The two drawings are identical in almost every respect except for the presence of a *pentimento* in the Woodner drawing indicating an alteration in the placement of the Palazzo Ducale in the left middleground. The Woodner drawing has suffered somewhat more over time. All the ink has soaked into the paper, diffusing the lines and washes, thereby making the overall information less legible.

As Ward points out, the Woodner drawing is particularly important in our understanding of the artist's occasional complex working method. The large drawing is composed of joined sheets and certain motifs have been cut out and laid down on the surface once they were drawn to the artist's satisfaction. Thus, given the probable degree of alteration and handling by the artist, a cleaner

87

drawing of record was necessary, particularly when it is understood that the actual completion of the painting would not be accomplished for yet another twenty years.

The compositional organization is typical of Federico's grand manner of setting his scenes of ceremony in impressive architectural surroundings. The abundance of *repoussoir* elements might, to some eyes, seem excessive (there are no less than eighteen men, women, children and animals directing one's vision to the narrative importance of the middleground). But by the 1580s this type of presentation had become a hallmark of Taddeo's posthumous influence and reflects Federico's inclination to build on his brother's inventions.

A related drawing for the kneeling woman in the foreground is at Christ Church, Oxford (0216). A head study of the same model is in Paris, Institut Néerlandais (1978 - T.14) and what might be an additional study of this figure is in Kansas City (see cat. no. 77).

For other historical and iconographical aspects of the commission see preceding entry.

EXHIBITED IN NEW YORK ONLY

FEDERICO ZUCCARO

88 *The Submission of Emperor Frederick Barbarossa to Pope Alexander III*, c. 1582?

Pen and ink with brown wash, partially squared for transfer in black chalk
525 x 455 mm. (20 ¾ x 18 inches)
The Woodner Family Collection, New York WD-135

PROVENANCE: Sale, Sotheby's London, 8 December 1972, lot 28.

LITERATURE: Goldner 1988, under no. 55.

EXHIBITIONS: Malibu 1983, no.25.

See preceding entry.

88

FEDERICO ZUCCARO

89 *Study of Two Male Figures*
verso: Boy Kneeling Before a Crucifix c. 1582

Inscribed on recto, lower right: *F. Zuccar*
Red chalk. Verso: red and black chalk
270 x 197 mm. (10 ¾ x 7 ¾ inches)
The Woodner Family Collection, New York WD-785

PROVENANCE: Jonathan Richardson, Sr. (Lugt 2184); John Barnard,
London (Lugt 1419); sale Sotheby's New York, 16 January 1985, lot 25.

LITERATURE: none

EXHIBITIONS: none

The *verso* figure of the young boy kneeling in prayer before a large crucifix was eventually used by Federico for the young praying boy in the center foreground of *The Submission of Frederick Barbarossa to Pope Alexander III* (fig.43) and is datable to around 1582 although it might have been made earlier and kept, as many of Federico's genre studies seem to have been, for future use. Thus, it may also date from the Florentine period of 1575-79 as its style indicates. Individual red and black chalk studies of the praying woman to the left of the boy survive in the collections at Christ Church, Oxford (0216) and the Lugt Collection (1978.t.14).

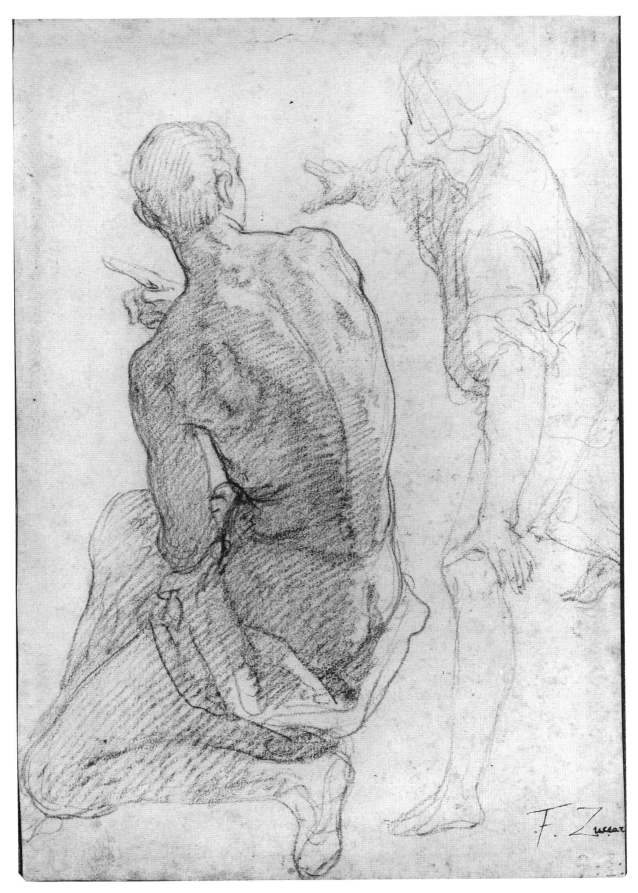

89 *recto*

89 *verso*

The repoussoir figure studies on the *recto* might relate to the figures in the right foreground of a drawing in the Louvre (4436) of *Saints Peter and the Disciples Praying to Decide whether Matthew or Barnabas will Replace Judas as an Apostle* of which there is an identical version at Windsor Castle (5197) and a variant in the Victoria and Albert Museum, London (Dyce 195, see Ward-Jackson 1979, no. 423). It is just as likely, however, that Federico used the partially draped nude model seen from behind in the Woodner drawing to work out more fully the pose of the figure in the lower left corner of the early sketch for *The Submission of Emperor Frederick Barbarossa to Pope Alexander III* in the Morgan Library (cat. no. 86). Here he changes only the position and gesture of the right arm. This figure was finaly omitted from the actual painting while the praying boy on the *verso* was included, thus indicating that this drawing was kept by the artist for future reference.

FEDERICO ZUCCARO

90 *A Pope Receiving a Dignitary in a Public Place* c. 1582

Inscribed on old mount in black ink, recto lower left: *Federigo Zucchero*;
lower center: *Public Rejoicing in a City*; lower right: *5 3/4 h.-11 w./Roscoe
No205/2*
Pen and ink with brown wash over black chalk
148 x 284 mm. (5 ⅞ x 11 inches)
The Art Institute of Chicago, Leonora Hall Gurley Memorial Collection
1922.1057

PROVENANCE: Roscoe; sale, Liverpool, 23-28 September 1816, lot 205;
Lord Stanley, Earl of Derby; F. Tate, London, (mark not in Lugt); sale 6-7
August 1914, Puttick and Simpson, London (mark not in Lugt); William
F.E. Gurley, Chicago (mark not in Lugt);Leonora Hall Gurley Memorial
Collection (Lugt supp. 1230b).

LITERATURE: Joachim and McCullagh 1979, no.34, pl.42.

EXHIBITIONS: Nielson 1972, no.15.

As Joachim and McCullagh have reasonably argued, this drawing would appear to have been executed by Federico at around the same time he was designing the *Submission of the Emperor Frederick Barbarossa to Alexander III*. While it is arranged horizontally rather than vertically like most of the other scenes in the series, it is quite similar in style to other studies for the commission, particularly that in the Pierpont Morgan Library (1973.29 cat. no. 86). In addition the composition is heavily weighted with repoussoir figures, a compositional mannerism that Federico found compelling during the 1570s and 1580s. It should be pointed out that the drawing is not necessarily related in a specific sense to the artist's commissions from this period and may be nothing more than a compositional *divertimento* worked out as something like a conceptual counterpoint to his actual task at this time.

As has also been pointed out, the setting is very Roman in appearance and it could relate to one of the complementary scenes in the Sala del Gran Consiglio. It is possible that this sketch was a first thought for one of the more horizontal compositions in that chamber, possibly for *The Coronation of Emperor Frederick Barbarossa by Pope Adrian*, originally painted by Tintoretto for the chamber, presumably copied by Federico (see cat. no. 54), but ultimately omitted by the artists who replaced the wall paintings after of the fire of 1577.

FEDERICO ZUCCARO

91 *Two Angels Supporting a Cartouche*

Pen and ink with brown wash over traces of black chalk
124 x 220 mm. (4 $^{11}/_{16}$ x 8 $^{11}/_{16}$ inches)
The Snite Museum of Art, University of Notre Dame on extended loan as a
promised gift from Mr. John D. Reilly, L85.45.28

PROVENANCE: John Minor Wisdom, Jr., New Orleans

LITERATURE: none

EXHIBITIONS: New Orleans 1981, no. 29; Weiner 1985, repr.; Spiro and
Coleman 1987, no. 23, repr.

Given the number of such figures executed in the sixteenth century in both stucco and paint, the odds against connecting this drawing with a specific project are rather great. It is, however, fully representative of Federico Zuccaro's later style.

The Notre Dame *Two Angels Supporting a Cartouche* calls to mind similar figures in stucco in the Sala d'Ercole at Caprarola villa of the Farnese (Faldi 1981, pp.224-25) and a drawing in the Louvre (4556) attributed to Federico. Also, in a private collection in Paris there is a drawing for an entire wall decoration featuring an equestrian monument in the center with paired engaged columns, niches and caryatid figures on either side (fig. 44). Above the mounted figure is a

fig. 44, Federico Zuccaro,
Design for a Wall Decoration,
Private Collection, Paris

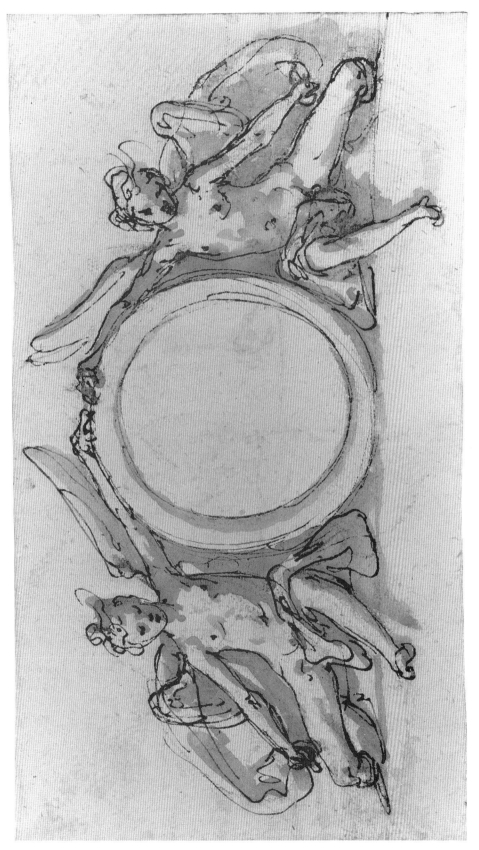

quickly sketched pair of *putti* holding an oval cartouche in poses similar to the Notre Dame sketch. A separate study for the mounted general alone is in the Louvre (112073, Gere 1969b, no. 97). The destination of this project remains unknown.

AFTER FEDERICO ZUCCARO

92 *Four Women with Musical Instruments and Another Figure*

Inscribed verso top center: *de. fred. Zuccaro.*
Pen and ink with gray-green wash
387 x 252 mm. (15 ¼ x 9 ¹⁵/₁₆ inches)
The Art Museum, Princeton University, Bequest of Dan Fellows Platt, 48-917.

PROVENANCE: H.Füssli and Co. (Lugt 1008); Dan Fellows Platt (Lugt supp. 750a).

LITERATURE: Gibbons 1977, no. 707.

EXHIBITIONS: none

This drawing exists in two versions. The second, approximately ten millimeters smaller, in the Fitzwilliam Museum, Cambridge (3185-6), was etched in reverse by Jan de Bisschop as no.42 in his *Paradigmata Graphices* (Van Gelder 1971, p. 284, figs. 71 and 72) in the year 1671. The etching carries the inscription *Fred. Zuccaro inv.* and the Fitzwilliam drawing *Frederico Zuccharo. Fecit 1608*. The cataloguer of the Princeton drawings mistakenly lists this drawing as "After Taddeo Zuccaro" working it seems from a recollection by Jacob Bean, noted on the mat, that the Cambridge drawing was by Taddeo.

Although the date on the Fitzwilliam drawing would argue against it, it is possible that the group of musicians is a more fully worked out version of the muses taken from the left hand group sketched out in the Chapel Hill composition (cat. no. 47). Is it possible, given its more finished appearance, that the Princeton sheet is a copy after the final look of a portion of the fresco in the home of Stefano Margani, noted by Vasari and executed in the late 1550s?

The authorship of the Princeton drawing presents a number of problems. First, the Cambridge and Princeton drawings are practically identical in size, medium and style. Second, the use of gray-brown wash in the Cambridge version and gray-green wash in the Princeton drawing seem more characteristic of the choice of a Netherlandish artist rather than an Italian one. Jan de Bisschop used a number of drawings as models for his series of etchings but he was also in the

92

habit of copying paintings and sculpture he saw in the course of his travels. Thus, the possible authorship of de Bisschop for one or the other version of this composition should not be ruled out as an option, the inscription regarding Federico could have been used as an *aide-memoire* by the copyist and not necessarily as a means of identifying the hand responsible for the drawing itself.

FEDERICO ZUCCARO

93 *Study of an Escutcheon*
verso: *Two Studies of Escutcheons*

Pen and ink with wash over red chalk, heightened with white
173 x 139 mm. (6 ¹³⁄₁₆ x 5 ½ inches)
Cooper-Hewit Museum, The Smithsonian Institution's National Museum
of Design, New York, 1938-88-2608

PROVENANCE: Giovanni Piancastelli; Mr. and Mrs. Edward D.
Brandegee.

LITERATURE: none

EXHIBITIONS: none

In 1610, Pierre Firens published in Paris twenty-two engravings of cartouches designed by Federico Zuccaro. While there are some general areas of similarity with this drawing, it was probably not intended for that purpose. It has, nevertheless, the look of a fairly late study by Federico although clearly a very different sort of drawing than cat. no. 91 of virtually the same subject. In many respects, it should be noted that much of Taddeo's manner of expression survives in this drawing, which makes even the assertion of a late date open to considerable doubt.

93

FEDERICO ZUCCARO

94 *Trinity Surrounded by Angels* 1592-95

Inscribed lower left in ink: *tadeus Succarus*
341 x 252 mm. (13 ⅞ x 9 ⅞ inches)
National Gallery of Canada, Ottawa, 9975 P.29

PROVENANCE: Purchased in 1963 from W.R. Jeudwine, London.

LITERATURE: Popham and Fenwick 1965, pp. 33-34, no. 44; Macandrew
1980, p. 82 under no. 755b.

EXHIBITIONS: *Exhibition of Old Master Drawings*, W.R. Jeudwine, London,
1963, no. 3, pl.11; Washington, D. C. 1988, pp. 31-33, no. 6.

The history and function of this drawing has recently been recounted by
David McTavish in his excellent entry in the exhibition of drawings from
the National Gallery of Canada (Washington D. C. 1988, pp. 31-33). The
important points are that this drawing, first recognized as a work by Federico by
Philip Pouncey, is a preliminary design for the cupola of the Cappella degli
Angeli in the church of the Gesù in Rome commissioned and executed between
1592-95. The subject is the *Assumption of the Virgin* and *The Trinity.* Federico's
point of departure for the *Assumption* was his solution for the completion of that
scene in the Pucci Chapel (see cat. no. 46).

There are a number of differences between the Ottawa drawing and the
finished painting, primarily in the pose of the Virgin, the alteration of the
number of figures and placement of the Trinity, and the arrangement of the
many angels. McTavish has noted that the clouds that spill over the enframing
device in the Ottawa drawing, while absent in the fresco itself, become of
interest considering the later *tour de force* in the same church by Giovanni Battista
Gaulli. There, a century later, one finds a similar negation of any confinement of
the subject within a traditional frame, only this time on a grand scale.

A related drawing is in the Ashmolean Museum, Oxford (755b, cf. Macandrew
1980, p. 82).

94

FEDERICO ZUCCARO

95 *Study for an Assumption of the Virgin*
verso: *Another Study for the Assumption*

Pen and ink with brown wash
160 x 126 mm. (6 ¼ x 5 inches)
Jak Katalan, New York

PROVENANCE: unknown

LITERATURE: none

EXHIBITIONS: none

This drawing, recently acquired on the art market, carries an attribution to Taddeo Zuccaro and is thought to relate to his *Assumption* in the Pucci Chapel, S. Trinità dei Monti, Rome. While this seems logical to some degree, the mitten-like hands, the attenuation of the figure and the heavy use of wash are all indications of Federico's style at a rather late moment. Gere (letter of 30 March 1989) sees certain features suggestive of Taddeo in the drawing but supposes it is likely the work of Federico.

There are a number of puzzling aspects and connections regarding the drawing's composition or what can be inferred from what is obviously only a fragment of a larger sketch. The pose of the Virgin, while not reflecting that of the *Assumption* in the Pucci Chapel, does resemble that in the altarpiece by Francesco Bassano above the high altar in the church of S. Luigi dei Francesi in Rome, painted between 1585-90 (see Edoardo Arslan, *I Bassano*, Milan, 1960, vol. 1, p.202). This painting was copied by Jacob Matham in 1611, accurately reflecting the lower half of the composition while substantially changing the upper half. The work was, at that time, incorrectly attributed to Taddeo Zuccaro (fig. 45; see Gere 1966a, p. 289, n.11). That attribution is understandable considering the very close relationship of the lower section of the composition to that of Taddeo's composition, as well. That the Katalan drawing is by Bassano is, however, not likely. The relationship to the Pucci chapel is made more confusing by virtue of Federico's participation in it.

A second possibility worth considering is that the drawing was a first thought for the pose of the Virgin, carried aloft by angels, in the domed ceiling of the Capella degli Angeli in the Gesù by designed by Federico in the mid-1590s (see

95

previous entry). The pose and manner of description of the upper body of the Virgin and the background of cherubim arranged in concentric bands suggested in the Katalan drawing seem to find analogies in the Ottawa drawing.

If the drawing is by Federico, then the style would certainly place it in the period of the execution of the Gesù fresco. However, Federico was always capable of a large degree of self-quotation and exercised the ability to re-cycle much of his and Taddeo's imagery into the late commissions.

fig. 45, Jacob Matham (after Taddeo Zuccaro?), *Assumption of the Virgin*, The Metropolitan Museum of Art, The Elisha Whittelsey Collection, The Elisha Whittelsey Fund, 1951

280

FEDERICO ZUCCARO

96 *Taddeo Zuccaro Entering Rome with Disegno and Spirito* c. 1590-95

Inscribed lower left and right borders, in an old hand: *nato del 1519* and
morto del 1566 and in lower right: *e.22*
Pen and ink with brown wash
270 x 184 mm. (10 ½ x 7 ¼ inches)
Private Collection, Montreal and Toronto

PROVENANCE: Padre Sebastiano Resta, Milan (Lugt 2992); F. Abott,
Edinburgh (Lugt 970); Emile Wauters, Paris (Lugt 911); Colnaghi, 1971.

LITERATURE: Colnaghi, *Old Master Drawings*, London, 1971, cat. no. 16, pl. V.

EXHIBITIONS: Taylor 1976, no.4.

The history of Federico's series of the *Life of Taddeo* is, perhaps, best summarized in the recent publication by Sotheby's and John Gere (forthcoming 1990). The salient points can be quickly summarized, however.

At some point after the death of Taddeo, Federico Zuccaro planned a series of twenty-four allegorical and narrative scenes tracing the important moments of his brother's artistic career. It has been assumed by most previous writers (for example Körte, 1935, pp.68-70; Heikamp 1957, p.175ff;and Leopold 1979, pp.312-362) that the series was intended as a decoration for a room in the Palazzo Zuccaro. The series followed the following order:

1. Allegory of Faith and Religion.
2. Taddeo departs for Rome
3. Minerva shows Taddeo Rome.
4. Taddeo is met at Rome's Gates by Servitude, Discomfort and Fatigue.
5. Taddeo is rejected as an apprentice by Francesco da' Sant Agnolo.
6. Allegory of Patience and Labor.
7. Taddeo is apprenticed to Giovampiero Calavrese.
8. Taddeo is sent on errands by Calavrese's wife.
9. Taddeo draws by moonlight in the Calavrese home.
10. Taddeo does menial household chores for Calavrese's wife.
11. Allegory of Intelligence and Labor.
12. Taddeo copies from Raphael's Chigi Palace loggia.
13. Taddeo falls ill and dreams of a Polidoro façade.
14. Ill, Taddeo returns to his parents.

nato del 1519

morto del 1566

15. Cured, Taddeo returns to Rome and is welcomed by Spiritual Values and
    Drawing.
16. Allegory of Study and Intelligence.
17. Taddeo draws from the Laocoön and Raphael's Vatican Stanze.
18. Taddeo copies Michelangelo's *Last Judgment*.
19. Taddeo copies a Roman relief and a Polidoro façade.
20. Taddeo frescoes the Palazzo Mattei and is admired by Michelangelo,
    Daniele da Volterra, Giorgio Vasari, Francesco Salviati and others.

There then followed allegorical portraits of Taddeo and his artistic precursors Michelangelo, Raphael, and Polidoro.

The drawings exist in what is assumed to be the original set (once in the A.W.S. Rosenbach Library, Philadelphia, later owned by the British Rail Pension Fund and presently on the art market) and a number of replicas and copies. These are best, but not comprehensively, charted in Leopold. It should not be assumed that other versions of these scenes are necessarily the product of assistants and followers.

This drawing in a Canadian private collection portrays the fifteenth moment in the cycle when, cured of his illness, Taddeo returns to Rome and is welcomed by the personifications of *disegno* and *spirito*. Waiting for him on the other side of the gates are the three graces. This is, essentially, the moment where Taddeo's fortunes finally take a turn for the better. After enduring many hardships as a youth (Federico's morality play for artists seems predicated on the notion of "paying one's dues") and overcoming huge obstacles, this last set of scenes demonstrates the dividends of study and intelligence (illustrated by the allegories that follow) and following the models of the great masters. The moment when Taddeo re-enters Rome is the beginning of his artistic victories which reach their climax in the last scene where the Roman artistic establishment, including the aged Michelangelo, admire one of Taddeo's early commissions, the painted façade of the Palazzo Mattei.

Federico worked frequently with the notion of the uphill battle that results in achievement. This idea was often expressed in allegorical or metaphorical visual language. The hero is frequently accompanied by allegorical spirits that insure his success whether in prints, drawings or palace frescoes (for more on this subject see Hermann-Fiore 1979, pp.49-51).

The differences between the ex-Rosenbach/British Rail drawing (fig. 46) and this one are few but possibly meaningful. First, the Canadian version seems to have been cut down a bit, the entire upper and part of the lower foils of the cartouche having been trimmed. Second, the figures in both drawings are labeled, very legibly in block capitals in the ex-Rosenbach/British Rail example, quickly and somewhat awkwardly in the Canadian version, the words *Tadeo* and *Grazia* gone over twice and corrected. Finally, the ex-Rosenbach/British Rail drawing is more richly and fully worked with brown wash than the Canadian version. It is not impossible that the same hand executed both drawings and it is quite certain that Federico, in typical fashion, made sketches as working drawings and drawings of record in this instance as in others.

Six of the series, including this scene, were painted by an assistant and are now in the Palazzo Venezia, Rome. A version in pen and ink is also in the Uffizi (11018). A lithograph of the scene was executed by Jean Baptiste Mauzaisse.

fig. 46, Federico Zuccaro,
Taddeo Zuccaro is met by Spirito and Disegno at the Gates to Rome,
New York, art market

FEDERICO ZUCCARO

97 *Self-Portrait*

Red and black chalk
143 x 103 mm. (5 ⅝ x 4 inches)
The Pierpont Morgan Library, New York, IV, 171

PROVENANCE: Marquis of Normandy; Charles Fairfax Murray; J. Pierpont Morgan, purchased, 1910.

LITERATURE: Morgan, John Pierpont. *Collection J. Pierpont Morgan. Drawings by the old masters. Formed by C. Fairfax Murray*, London, 1905-19, IV, no. 171.

EXHIBITIONS: Gealt 1983, no. 12, repr.

97

W hile not inscribed or otherwise identified as a self-portrait of Federico, this drawing is close enough in appearance with other portraits of the artist to permit this identification (see Hermann-Fiore 1979, pp. 68-69, figs. 23-25 for examples), particularly that of himself with his wife, Francesca, in the Sala Terrena of the Palazzo Zuccaro. It is conceivable that the present portrait dates from this time, thereby making him in his mid-to-late fifties. The handling of the chalks is consistent in style with other sketches for this project, particularly those in Berlin (Kupferstichkabinett, 18451) and the Louvre (4573).

Also supporting evidence in suggesting a possible use in the Palazzo Zuccaro project is the gentlemanly gesture Federico adopts in the Morgan drawing, a mannered pose in keeping with that in the fresco. In his last years Federico began to receive the respect he always thought was his due. This portrait, quick in execution and laden with intensity, is a testimony to his stature as artist and gentleman.

FEDERICO ZUCCARO

98 *View of St. Peter's*
verso: *Study of a Young Man* c. 1598

Inscribed on strip of paper attached to bottom of sheet: *Vue de St. Pierre de Rome...Tiré du Cabinet de Monsieur le Marquis de Gouvernet 2*
Red chalk. Verso: red and black chalk
255 x 407 mm. (10 x 16 inches)
The J. Paul Getty Museum, Malibu 85.GB.228

PROVENANCE: Marquis de Gouvernet, Paris; private collection, Paris; art market, Zurich.

LITERATURE: Goldner 1988, no.55, repr.

Although Federico was not known for his interest in landscape and city views, he was a sensitive observer of the world around him and did, on occasion, go sketching for the pure enjoyment of it. In this he differs from his brother for whom, as for Michelangelo, landscape held no interest whatsoever. Federico's sketches of Rome, Florence and Vallombrosa are invariably executed in chalk.

98 verso

Goldner has presented a good case for dating this sketch of St. Peter's to around 1590 based on the appearance on the left of a portion of the Egyptian obelisk placed by order of Pope Sixtus V in 1586. Also visible in this view of the front of St. Peter's are from left to right, the archiepiscopal palace, the old façade of the cathedral with its triple portal with the guards' bastion before it, the three storied benediction loggia and the Vatican Palace. The artist has lightly sketched the statues of Saints Peter and Paul at the bottom of the staircase.

It is possible that the drawing dates several years later. The *verso* portrays a sketch of a young man who bears a strong resemblance to Girolamo Zuccaro, Federico's youngest son. Together with his three brothers, he is portrayed in the lower left in one of the lunettes of the Sala Terrena in the Palazzo Zuccaro painted by Federico in 1598 (Körte 1935, p.77). While not conclusive evidence, the similarity suggests that the sheet might well date to this later period in Federico's career. Another preliminary sketch also in red and black chalks for this entire group is in the Berlin Kupferstichkabinett (18451). Its execution is rougher than the portrait on the Getty sheet yet more in keeping with the style found in the sketch of St. Peter's.

Several other drawings of presumably Roman ruins in the Louvre (4627,4628 and 4629) are probably related to the Getty drawing.

EXHIBITED IN NEW YORK ONLY

FEDERICO ZUCCARO

99 *The Canonization of Saint Hyacinth by Pope Clement VIII* c. 1600
verso: *Studies for the Canonization of Saint Hyacinth*

Inscribed on recto lower right in Crozat's hand:*69* and *F.Zuccaro.*; on verso lower right in Crozat's hand: *70* and *7/2 ff. avec Sainte(?)* and center *V pt. 67* and *220*.
Pen and ink with brown wash. Watermark: bird (similar to Briquet 12158)
Rome 1592-93
174 x 252 mm. (6 ¾ x 10 inches)
Private Collection, New Haven

PROVENANCE: Pierre Crozat, Paris (Lugt 2951); Jean Murraceilole

LITERATURE: none

EXHIBITIONS: none

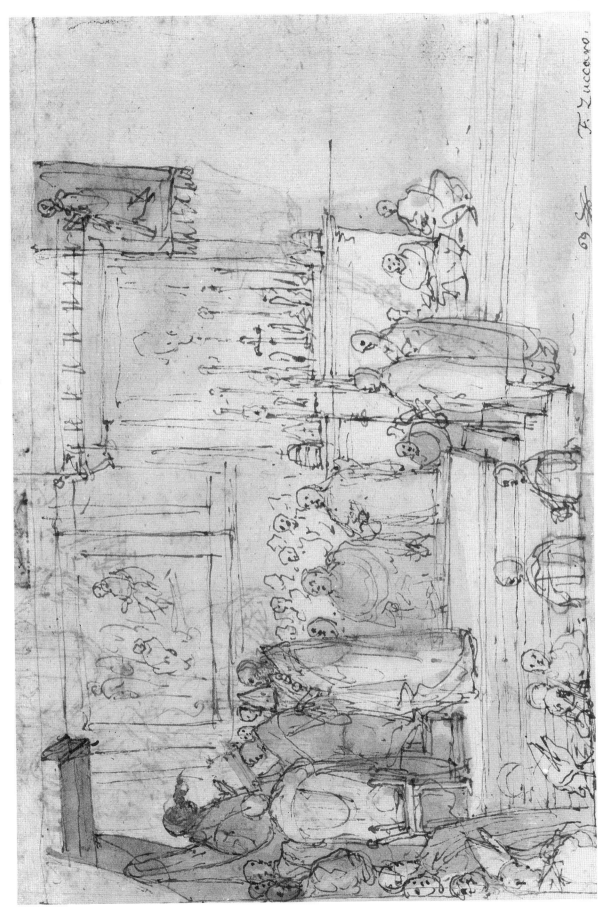

F. Zuccaro.

99 recto

99 *verso*

This highly important two-sided sheet of studies records Federico's first thoughts for his fresco on the right hand wall of the Saint Hyacinth chapel in the church of S. Sabina, Rome built by the then prior of the church Girolamo Bernerio, Cardinal of Ascoli (fig. 47). The moment represented would have been a recent one for Federico. Hyacinth (or Jacek) of Cracow (1185-1257) was a Dominican friar canonized in 1594 by Pope Clement VIII. Federico signed and dated the frescoed vault, portraying the *Apotheosis of Saint Hyacinth*, in the Jubilee Year 1600.

The New Haven drawing joins other preparatory designs for this commission in a Parisian private collection (illus. in Gere 1971, fig. 37); the Pierpont Morgan Library (cat. no. 100); and the Ecole des Beaux-Arts, Paris (441, though weak in execution, not necessarily a copy as suggested by Gere). This listing is also the sequence in which they were executed in all probability. The Ecole des Beaux-Arts sheet is the last and closest to the final painting and the only one that lists some of the participants.

Apparently one area of the composition that gave the artist some degree of trouble was the placement of the Pope in relationship to the entreating cardinals and other clergy. Federico explored different options for the posture of the Pope, portraying him on the New Haven sheet both standing and seated. He would be shown seated in the drawing in the Parisian collection and the fresco, although standing in the Morgan Library and Ecole des Beaux-Arts drawings. Federico also changed his mind several times on the shape and length of the platform on which the baldachin is placed, using a short platform in most of the drawings but extending its dimensions in the final painting. The foreground repoussoir figures also went through a number of changes before he decided on a combination of figures looking both out at the viewer and in at the event.

fig. 47, Federico Zuccaro, *The Canonization of St. Hyacinth*, S. Sabina, Rome

FEDERICO ZUCCARO

100 *The Canonization of Saint Hyacinth by Pope Clement VIII* c. 1600

Inscribed on verso in pen and ink: *115*
Pen and ink with brown wash, heightened with white on blue paper,
squared for transfer in black chalk
261 x 375 mm (10 ⅜ x 14 ¾ inches)
The Pierpont Morgan Library, New York, The Janos Scholz Collection
1973.30

PROVENANCE: Ottaviano Zuccaro (?); Savoia-Aosta (Lugt supp. 47a);
Janos Scholz, New York.

LITERATURE: Ryskamp 1984, p.186.

EXHIBITIONS: Staten Island 1961, no. 35; New York 1971, no. 99; Norton
1971; Oberhuber and Walker 1973, no. 12, repr.

This is a more highly evolved version of the composition described in the previous entry. The size of the composition is expanded and more figures are included in various poses.

Heikamp (1967, p.65, n.43) cites a published inventory of a number of drawings left by Federico to his son Ottaviano dated 14 June 1610 among which is "Una canonizzazione in carta azzurra."

FEDERICO ZUCCARO

101 *The Lamentation with Six Angels and Two other Figures*

Pen and ink with brown wash heightened with white on gray-green paper
318 x 221 mm. (12 ½ x 8 ¾ inches)
The Art Museum, Princeton University, Gift of Frank Jewett Mather, 47-150

PROVENANCE: Frank Jewett Mather, Jr. (Lugt supp. 1853a)

LITERATURE: Gibbons 1977, I, p.216, no.702.

EXHIBITIONS: New York 1930, no.35.

This composition is derived from Taddeo's easel painting in the Borghese Gallery, Rome (fig. 48). A slightly smaller version exists in a European private collection. However, the rather rough and scratchy use of pen and ink and the heavy application of white heightening to the figures suggest that this drawing dates quite late in Federico's career. Aspects of its execution suggest other late drawings such as those in Worcester (cat. no. 103) and Santa Barbara (cat. no. 102).

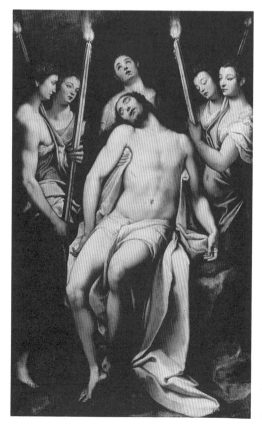

fig. 48, Taddeo Zuccaro,
Dead Christ,
Galleria Borghese, Rome

101

We know from the inventory left behind at his death that Federico frequently portrayed the subject of the Pietà, for which this type of subject might have qualified in the eyes of the person preparing such a list of works of art. No fewer than six such paintings are mentioned in the document (Körte 1935 pp.83-84). We also know from his book *Passaggio* that Federico painted a fresco of a *Pietà with Four Angels, the Virgin and St. Bernard* for a chapel on one of the Borromean Islands on Lago Maggiore in 1604 (Körte 1935, p.78). Although the Princeton sketch shows six rather than four angels and the monastic figure cannot with certainty be identified as St. Bernard, it is possible that the drawing was an early idea for the fresco.

The drawing's relationship to Federico's earlier work, particularly the *Trinity* in Boston and *Christ Supported by Angels* in New Haven has already been mentioned. In its conception, this presentation of the *Dead Christ* with angels bearing large tapers may also be linked to Rosso Fiorentino's great painting of the same subject in the Museum of Fine Arts, Boston. It was not unusual, however, for Federico to return to some successful early creations when seeking inspiration during his last years.

FEDERICO ZUCCARO

102 *Resurrection of Christ*

Pen and ink with brown wash heightened with white on tan paper
338 x 278 mm. (13 $^5/_{16}$ x 10 $^{15}/_{16}$ inches)
University Art Museum, Santa Barbara, gift of the Lorser Feitelson and Helen Lundeberg Feitelson Arts Foundation to the University Art Museum, Santa Barbara.

PROVENANCE: London collection (see Moir 1983, no. 24).

LITERATURE: none

EXHIBITIONS: Moir 1983; *Old Master Drawings from the Collection of the University Art Museum, Santa Barbara*, Haggerty Museum of Art, Marquette University, Milwaukee 1988, checklist, no. 16.

102

ormerly attributed to Taddeo, this drawing has recently and rightly been assigned to Federico. Moir (1983, no. 24) suggests an early date around 1572 by comparison with a sketch for Federico's *Calumny of Apelles*, engraved by Cort in that year. While this is possible, given the life of the line and general energy in the spidery use of the pen, it seems more sound to see this as a late example of Federico's work. In this respect it is more in stylistic sympathy with the *David and Goliath* at Worcester (cat. no. 103) or, even, the small allegorical figure of *Faith* in New Haven (cat. no. 104). Whatever the case, the Santa Barbara drawing has all the triumphant feel of a strongly post-Tridentine work well into the Baroque age. In this regard it is also in keeping with late commissions such as the chapels in the Gesù and S. Sabina.

FEDERICO ZUCCARO

103 *David and Goliath*

Pen and ink with gray wash on faded blue paper
224 x 286 mm. (8 ⅝ x 11 ¼ inches)
Worcester Art Museum, Worcester, Massachusetts 1956.34

PROVENANCE: H.M. Calmann, London.

LITERATURE: Vey 1958, p. 65, no. 117; McTavish 1985, p. 56.

EXHIBITIONS: H. M. Calmann, London, 1953, no. 13.

While it is tempting to connect this drawing with that of the same subject in the collection of Duke Ferretti (cat. no. 82, from c. 1580) owing to the rarity of this subject in Federico's *oeuvre*, from all stylistic criteria, the Worcester sketch should be dated quite late in Federico's career. In this regard, it should be viewed as stemming from the same period as the *Lamentation with Six Angels, the Virgin and a Monastic Saint* at Princeton (cat. no. 101).

FEDERICO ZUCCARO

104 *Allegorical Figure of Faith* c. 1604

Inscribed lower center: .... *di Taddeo*
Pen and ink with brown wash
69 x 263 mm. (2 ¾ x 10 ⅜ inches)
Yale University Art Gallery, New Haven, Everett V. Meeks Fund, 1963.9.30

PROVENANCE: W.B. Jeudwine, London; purchased 1963.

LITERATURE: Haverkamp-Begemann and Logan 1970, I, p. 157, no. 279.

EXHIBITIONS: none

This drawing is typical of many of Federico's quick, late pen sketches for an architectural ornamentation that would include a number of allegorical figures interspersed throughout a decorative program. This figure of faith, holding a chalice and cross, cannot be associated with a specific project but is similar in pose and composition to two other drawings of similar reclining figures attributed to Federico in the Louvre (4474 and 4474 bis). Of all Federico's commissions it most resembles the figures in the medallions in the Hall of the Zodiac in the Palazzo Marozzi, Pavia (Pinetti 1924, p.616). Thus, the dating should be placed during the time of this commission, around 1604.

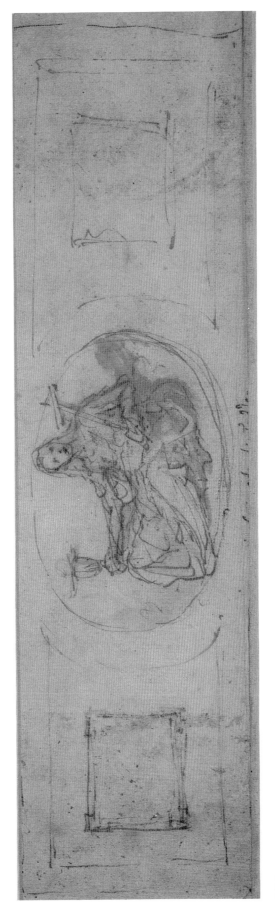

BIBLIOGRAPHY

Aarhus 1973
> *Mestertegningen fra Chatsworth*. Aarhus Kunstmuseum, 1973.

Alasko 1983
> Alasko, Richard Raymond. *Religious Narrative in Sixteenth Century Rome*. The Snite Museum of Art, University of Notre Dame, 1983.

Amherst 1974
> *Major Themes in Roman Baroque Art from Regional Collections*. Mead Art Building, Amherst, 1974.

Andrews 1968
> Andrews, Keith. *National Gallery of Scotland, Catalogue of Italian Drawings*. 2 vols., Cambridge, 1968.

Apolloni 1978
> Apolloni, W. *Dai Manieristi ai Neoclassici, Disegni Italiani*. Rome, 1978.

Baglione
> Baglione, Giovanni. *Le vite de' Pittori, Scultori e Architetti*. Rome, 1935 (facsimile of 1652 edition)

Bartsch
> Bartsch, Adam. *Le Peintre-Graveur*. 21 vols. Vienna, 1803-1821.

Bartsch-Bohlin
> *The Illustrated Bartsch*. Vol. 39, *Italian Masters of the Sixteenth Century*, edited by Diane de Grazia Bohlin. New York, 1980.

Baumgart and Biagetti 1934
> Baumgart, Fritz and Biagio Biagetti. *Affreschi di Michelangelo, di Sabbatini, e F. Zuccari nella Cappella Paolina*. Vatican City, 1934.

Bean 1963
> Bean, Jacob. "Form and Function in Italian Drawings: Observations on Several New Acquisitions." *Metropolitan Museum of Art Bulletin* 21 (March 1963), 225-239.

Bean and Stampfle 1965
> Bean, Jacob and Felice Stampfle. *Drawings from New York Collections I: The Italian Renaissance*. The Metropolitan Museum of Art, New York, 1965.

Bean 1966
> Bean, Jacob. *Italian Drawings in the Art Museum*. Art Museum, Princeton University, 1966.

Bean 1968
> Bean, Jacob. "Drawings." (Annual Report) *Metropolitan Museum of Art Bulletin* 26 (October 1968), 85-87.

Bean and McKendry, 1969
> Bean, Jacob and John J. McKendry. "A Fortunate Year." *Metropolitan Museum of Art Bulletin* 27 (February 1969), 312-313.

Bean 1982
> Bean, Jacob. *15th and 16th Century Italian Drawings in the Metropolitan Museum of Art*. Metropolitan Museum of Art, New York, 1982.

Berendson 1970

    Berendson, Olga. "Taddeo Zuccaro's Paintings for Charles V's Obsequies in Rome." *The Burlington Magazine* 112 (December 1970), 809-810.

Bertini 1958

    Bertini, Aldo. *I Disegni italiani della Biblioteca Reale di Torino*. Rome, 1958.

Bierens de Haan 1948

    J.C.J. Bierens de Haan. *L'oeuvre gravé de Cornelis Cort*. The Hague, 1948.

Bora 1978

    Bora, Giulio. *I disegni del Codice Resta*. Milan, 1978.

Briquet 1907

    Briquet, G.M. *Les filigranes, dictionnaire historique des marques de papier*. 4 vols., Paris, 1907

Buchowiecki 1970

    Buchowiecki, Walthar. *Handbuch der Kirchen Roms*. 4 vols., Vienna, 1970

Byam Shaw 1969-1973

    Byam Shaw, James. *Old Master Drawings from Chatsworth*. National Gallery, Washington, D.C., 1969; Victoria and Albert Museum, London, 1973.

Byam Shaw 1972

    Byam Shaw, James. *Old Master Drawings from Christ Church, Oxford*. International Exhibitions Foundation, 1972-1973.

Byam Shaw 1976

    Byam Shaw, James. *Drawings by Old Masters at Christ Church, Oxford*, 2 vols. Oxford, 1976.

Byam Shaw 1983

    Byam Shaw, James. *The Italian Drawings of the Fritz Lugt Collection*, 3 vols. Institut Néerlandais, Paris, 1983.

Cambridge 1962

    Anxiety and Elegance - The Human Figure in Italian Art 1520-1580. Fogg Art Museum, Harvard University, Cambridge, 1962.

Cambridge 1979

    Old Master Drawings from the Charles A. Loeser Bequest. Fogg Art Museum, Harvard University, Cambridge, 1979.

Cambridge 1985

    Master Drawings from the Woodner Collection. Fogg Art Museum, Harvard University, Cambridge, 1985.

Chapel Hill 1969

    First Decade of Collection Exhibition. The William Hayes Ackland Memorial Art Center, Chapel Hill, 1969.

Cheney 1981

    Cheney, Iris. "Les premières décorations: Daniele de Volterra, Salviati et les frères Zuccari." *La Palais Farnese, Ecole française de Rome*. I, no. 1 (1981), 243-267.

Cheney 1981

    Cheney, Iris. "Catalogue of Preparatory Drawings Related to the Mid-Sixteenth-century Decorations in Palazzo Farnese." *Mélanges de l'Ecole Française de Rome* 93 (1981), 791-820.

Ciccarese 1986

    Ciccarese, Alessandra. "Documenti su Federico Zuccaro." *Storia dell'Arte* 58 (1986), 205.

Coffin 1960

    Coffin, David R. *The Villa d'Este at Tivoli*. Princeton, 1960.

Collobi 1938
:   Collobi, Licia. "Taddeo e Federico Zuccari nel Palazzo Farnese a Caprarola." *Critica d'arte* 3 (1938), 3, 70 ff.

Cologne 1963
:   *Italienische Meisterzeichnungen...Die Sammlung Janos Scholz.* Wallraf-Richartz Museum, Cologne, 1963-64.

Columbus 1961
:   *The Renaissance Image of Man and the World.* Columbus Museum of Art, 1961.

Davidson 1986
:   Davidson, Gail S. *Drawing the Fine Line: Discovering European Drawings in Long Island Private Collections.* Hillwood Art Gallery, Long Island University, 1986.

Denison and Mules 1981
:   Denison, Cara D. and Helen B. Mules. *European Drawings 1375-1825.* The Pierpont Morgan Library, New York, 1981.

Eiche 1984
:   Eiche, Sabine. "Francesco Maria II della Rovere as a patron of architecture and his villa at Monte Berticchio." *Mitteilungen des kunsthistorischen Institutes in Florenz* 27, no. 2 (1984), 77-108.

Emiliani 1975
:   Emiliani, Andrea. *Mostra di Federico Barocci.* Museo Civico, Bologna, 1975.

Emiliani 1985
:   Emiliani, Andrea, *Federico Barocci.* 2 vols., Bologna, 1985.

Emison 1987
:   Emison, Patricia A. *The Art of Teaching: Sixteenth-Century Allegorical Prints and Drawings.* Yale University Art Gallery, New Haven, 1986-87.

Faldi 1981
:   Faldi, Italo. *Il Palazzo Farnese di Caprarola.* Turin, 1981.

Feinblatt 1976
:   Feinblatt, Ebria. *Old Master Drawings from American Collections.* Los Angeles County Museum of Art, 1976.

Frerichs 1981
:   Frerichs, L.C.J. *Italiaanse Tekeningen II, de 15 en 16 Eeuw.* Rijksmuseum, Amsterdam, 1981.

Garzelli 1972
:   Garzelli, Annarosa. *Museo di Orvieto, Museo dell'Opera del Duomo.* Bologna, 1972.

Gealt 1983
:   Gealt, Adelheid. *Italian Portrait Drawings from North American Collections.* Indiana University Art Museum, Bloomington, 1983.

Gerards-Nelissen 1983
:   Gerards-Nelissen, Inemie. "Federigo Zuccaro and the Lament of Painting." *Simiolus* 13 (1983), 45-53.

Gere 1963a
:   Gere, John A. "Taddeo Zuccaro as a designer for maiolica." *The Burlington Magazine* 105 (July 1963), 306-315.

Gere 1963b
:   Gere, John A. "Two Panel Pictures by Taddeo Zuccaro and some related compositions, II: The Agony in the Garden in the Strossmayer Gallery, Zagreb.," *The Burlington Magazine* 105 (September 1963), 390-395.

Gere 1965
:   Gere, John A. "The Decoration of the Villa Giulia." *The Burlington Magazine* 107 (April

1965), 199ff.

Gere 1966a

Gere, John A. "Two Of Taddeo Zuccaro's last commissions, completed by Federico Zuccaro. "I. The Pucci Chapel in S. Trinità dei Monti," and "II. The high altar-piece in S. Lorenzo in Damaso." *The Burlington Magazine* 108 (March 1966), 286-293; (July 1966), 341-345.

Gere 1966b

Gere, John A. *Mostra di disegni degli Zuccari*. Gabinetto Disegni e Stampe degli Uffizi, Florence, 1966.

Gere 1969a

Gere, John A. *Taddeo Zuccaro: His Development Studied in His Drawings*. Chicago, 1969.

Gere 1969b

Gere, John A. *Dessins de Taddeo et Federico Zuccaro*. Cabinet des Dessins, Musée du Louvre, Paris, 1969.

Gere 1970

Gere, John A. "The Lawrence-Phillips-Rosenbach Zuccaro Album." *Master Drawings* 8 (Summer 1970), 123-140.

Gere 1971

Gere, John A. *I Disegni dei Maestri - il manierismo a Roma*. Milan, 1971.

Gere and Pouncey 1983

Gere, John A. and Philip Pouncey with Rosalind Wood. *Italian Drawings in the Department of Prints and Drawings in the British Museum - Artists working in Rome, c. 1550- c. 1660*. 2 vols. London, 1983.

Gibbons 1977

Gibbons, Felton L. *Catalogue of Italian Drawings in the Art Museum, Princeton University*. 2 vols., Princeton, 1977.

Goldner 1988

Goldner, George R. *European Drawings . 1 Catalogue of the Collections*. The J. Paul Getty Museum, Malibu, 1988.

Hanover 1971

Selections from the Collection of Esther S. and Malcolm W. Bick, Italian Drawings. Hopkins Center, Dartmouth College, Hanover, 1971.

Harprath 1977

Harprath, Richard. *Italienische Zeichnungen des 16. Jahrhunderts aus eigenem Besitz*. Staatliche Graphische Sammlung, Munich, 1977.

Haverkamp-Begemann and Sharp 1964

Haverkamp-Begemann, Egbert and Ellen Sharp. *Italian Drawings from the Collection of Janos Scholz*. Yale University Art Gallery, New Haven, 1964.

Haverkamp-Begemann and Logan 1970

Haverkamp-Begemann, Egbert and Mary Logan. *European Drawings and Watercolors in the Yale University Art Gallery*. New Haven, 1970.

Heikamp 1957

Heikamp, Detlef. "Vicende di Federico Zuccari." *Rivista d'arte* 32 (1957), 175-232.

Heikamp 1958

Heikamp, Detlef. "Ancora su Federico Zuccari." *Rivista d'arte* 33 (1958), 45-50.

Heikamp 1967

Heikamp, Detlef. "Federico Zuccari a Firenze 1575-1579." *Paragone* 205 (March 1967), 44-68; 207 (May 1967), 1-34.

Held 1981

Held, Julius S. Review of *European Drawings 1375-1825 at the Morgan Library*. *Master*

Drawings 19 (1981), 177.

Herrman-Fiore 1979

Herrman-Fiore, Kristina. "Die Fresken Federico Zuccaris in seinem Römischen Kunstlerhaus." *Römisches Jahrbuch für Kunstgeschichte* 18 (1979), 36-112.

Hermann-Fiore 1982

Hermann-Fiore, Kristina. 'Disegno' and 'Giuditio,' allegorical drawings by Federico Zuccaro and Cherubino Alberti." *Master Drawings* 20 (Fall 1982), 247-256.

Hibbard 1972

Hibbard, Howard. "*Ut picturae sermones*: The First Painted Decorations of the Gesù." in Wittkower, Richard and Irma B. Jaffe, eds. *Baroque Art: The Jesuit Contribution*, New York, 1972.

Houston 1966

Builders and Humanists. University of St. Thomas Art Department, Houston, 1966.

Indianapolis 1954

Pontormo to Greco. The Age of Mannerism. The John Herron Art Museum, Indianapolis, 1954.

Jaffé 1965

Jaffé, Michael. "Rubens as a Collector of Drawings: Part Two." *Master Drawings* 3 (Spring 1965), 21-35.

Joachim and McCullagh 1978

Joachim, Harold and Suzanne Folds McCullagh. *Italian Drawings in the Art Institute of Chicago*. Chicago, 1979.

Körte 1932

Körte, Werner. "Verlorene Frühwerke des Federico Zuccari in Röm." *Mitteilungen des Kunsthistorischen Institutes in Florenz* 3 (January 1932), 518-529.

Körte 1935

Körte, Werner. *Der Palazzo Zuccari in Röm*. Leipzig, 1935.

Lanciarini 1893

Lanciarini, V. "Dei Pittori Taddeo e Federico Zuccari." *Nuova Rivista Misena* 6 (1893), 83-109; 117-143; 153-157.

Lazarus and Yassin

Lazarus, Diane and Robert A Yassin. "A Note on a Sixteenth-Century Italian Drawing." *The University of Michigan Museum of Art Bulletin* 7, no. 1 n.s. (1972-73), 1-6.

LeBlanc

LeBlanc, Charles. *Manuel de l'amateur d'estampes* 1-4, Paris, 1854-89.

Leopold 1980

Leopold, Nikia S.C. *Artists' Homes in Sixteenth Century Italy*. Baltimore, Johns Hopkins University (dissertation), 1979.

London 1836

The Lawrence Gallery: Fourth Exhibition. A Catalogue of one hundred original Drawings by il Parmigianino (nos. 1-50) and A. da Coreggio (nos. 51-100), collected by Sir. Thomas Lawrence. Messers. Woodburn's Gallery, London, 1836.

London 1968

Italian Drawings from the Collection of Janos Scholz. Arts Council of Great Britain, London, Liverpool and Edinburgh, 1968.

London 1987

Master Drawings from the Woodner Collection. Royal Academy of Arts, London, 1987.

Lugt

Lugt, Frits. *Les Marques de collections de dessins & d'estampes*. Amsterdam, 1921; *Supplement*, The Hague, 1956.

Macandrew 1980

Macandrew, Hugh. *Ashmolean Museum, Oxford: Catalogue of the Collection of Drawings. Vol. 3 Italian Schools: Supplement*. Oxford, 1980.

Macandrew 1983

Macandrew, Hugh. *Italian Drawings in the Museum of Fine Arts*. Boston, 1983.

Majskaja 1980

Majskaja, M. "Risunki Staryh Masterov V. Soobranii GMII." *Muzei* 1 (1980), 54-77.

Malibu 1983

Master Drawings from the Woodner Collection. The J. Paul Getty Museum, Malibu, 1983.

Malibu 1988

The J. Paul Getty Museum Journal. Vol. 16, 1988.

McTavish 1981

McTavish, David *et al. The Arts of Italy in Toronto Collections, 1300-1800*. Art Gallery of Ontario, Toronto, 1981-82.

McTavish 1985

McTavish, David. *Italian Drawings from the Collection of Duke Roberto Ferretti*. Art Gallery of Ontario, Toronto, 1985-1986.

Middeldorf 1939

Middeldorf, Ulrich. "Three Italian Drawings in Chicago." *Art in America* 27 (1939), 10-14.

Middletown 1969

Italian Master Drawings from the Collection of Janos Scholz. Davison Art Center, Wesleyan University, Middletown, 1969.

Moir 1986

Moir, Alfred. *Old Master Drawings from the Collection of John and Alice Steiner*. Santa Barbara Museum of Art, 1986.

Monbeig-Goguel 1972

Monbeig-Goguel, Catherine. *Vasari et son temps*. Musée du Louvre, Paris, 1972.

Mongan and Sachs 1940

Mongan, Agnes and Paul Sachs. *Drawings in the Fogg Museum of Art*. 3 vols. Cambridge, 1940.

Monte Carlo 1966

Catalogue de l'exposition des dessins italiens du XV au XVIIIe siècle de la Collection H. de Marignane. Palais des Congrès, Monte Carlo, 1966.

Mundy 1981

Mundy, E. James. *Master Drawings Rediscovered*, Mount Holyoke College Art Museum, South Hadley, Massachusetts, 1981.

Neuberger 1986

Neuberger, Susanne. "Zur Apsis der SS Quattro Coronati in Röm." *Storia dell'Arte* 58 (September-December 1986), 211-222.

New Orleans 1981

Master Drawings from a Private Collection. New Orleans Museum of Art, 1981.

New York 1930

Exhibition of Drawings by Old Masters from the Private Collection of Professor Frank Jewett Mather, Jr. Roerich Museum, New York, 1930.

New York 1965

Italian Drawings from the Collection of Janos Scholz. The Metropolitan Museum of Art, New York, 1965.

New York 1971

One Hundred Italian Drawings from the Fourteenth to the Eighteenth Centuries from the

Janos Scholz Collection. The New School Art Center, New York, 1971.

New York 1972
> *Drawings Recently Acquired 1969-1971.* The Metropolitan Museum of Art, New York, 1972.

New York 1979
> *XVI Century Drawings from the Robert Lehman Collection.* The Metropolitan Museum of Art, New York, 1979.

Nielson 1972
> Nielson, Nancy W. *Italian Drawings Selected from Mid-Western Collections.* The St. Louis Art Museum, 1972.

Norton 1971
> *Italian Renaissance Drawings from the Janos Scholz Collection.* Watson Art Center, Wheaton College, Norton, Massachusetts, 1971.

Notre Dame 1970
> *The Age of Vasari.* Art Gallery, University of Notre Dame, 1970.

Notre Dame 1980
> *Janos Scholz, Musician and Collector.* The Snite Museum of Art, O'Shaughnessy Galleries, University of Notre Dame, 1980.

Oakland 1959
> *Venetian Drawings, 1400-1630.* Mills College Art Gallery, Oakland, 1959.

Oberhuber 1977
> Oberhuber, Konrad. *Renaissance and Baroque Drawings from the Steiner Collection.* Fogg Art Museum, Harvard University, Cambridge, 1977.

Oberhuber 1979
> Oberhuber, Konrad, ed. *Old Master Drawings: Selections from the Charles A. Loeser Bequest.* Fogg Art Museum Handbooks, vol. 1, Harvard University, Cambridge, 1979.

Oberhuber and Walker 1973
> Oberhuber, Konrad and Dean Walker. *Sixteenth Century Drawings from the Collection of Janos Scholz.* The National Gallery of Art, Washington, D.C. and the Pierpont Morgan Library, New York, 1973-74.

Olzewski 1981
> Olzewski, Edward J. *The Draftsman's Eye.* The Cleveland Museum of Art, 1981. (catalogue for 1979 exhibition).

Paris 1962
> *Le dessin italien dans les collections hollandaises.* Institut Néerlandais, Paris, 1962.

Paris 1965
> *Le XVI Siècle Européen, Dessins du Louvre.* Paris Musée du Louvre, 1965.

Partridge 1971-1972
> Partridge, Loren W. "The Sala d'Ercole in the Villa Farnese at Caprarola." *Art Bulletin* 53 (December 1971), 467-486 (part I); (March 1972), 50-62 (part II).

Partridge 1978
> Partridge, Loren W. "Divinity and Dynasty at Caprarola: Perfect History in the Room of Farnese Deeds." *Art Bulletin* 60 (September 1978), pp. 499-530.

Perez Sanchez 1969
> Perez Sanchez, Alfonzo E. *Catalogo de la coleccion de Dibujos del Instituto Jovellanos de Gijon.* Madrid, 1969.

Pignatti 1974
> Pignatti, Terisio. *Venetian Drawings from American Collections.* International Exhibitions Foundation, Washington, D.C. 1974-75.

Pillsbury 1974

    Pillsbury, Edmund. "Two Drawings by Federico Zuccaro Done in Venice." *Yale University Art Gallery Bulletin* 25 (Summer 1974), 8-13.

Pillsbury and Caldwell 1974

    Pillsbury, Edmund P. and John Caldwell. *Sixteenth Century Italian Drawings: Form and Function.* Yale University Art Gallery, New Haven, 1974.

Pillsbury and Richards 1978

    Pillsbury, Edmund P. and Louise S. Richards. *The Graphic Art of Federico Barocci.* Cleveland Museum of Art and Yale University Art Gallery, New Haven, 1978.

Pinetti 1924

    Pinetti, Angelo. "Una figurazione inèdita dello zodiaco di Federico Zuccari." *Emporium* 60 (1924), 613-622.

Popham and Fenwick, 1965

    Popham, Arthur E. and Kathleen M. Fenwick. *European Drawings in the Collection of the National Gallery of Canada.* Toronto, 1965.

Popham 1971

    Popham, Arthur E. *Catalogue of the Drawings of Parmigianino.* 3 vols., New Haven/London, 1971.

Popham 1973

    Popham, Arthur E. *The Drawings of Parmigianino.* London, 1953.

Popham and Wilde 1949

    Popham, Arthur E. and Johannes Wilde. *The Italian Drawings of the XV and XVI Centuries at Windsor Castle.* London, 1949.

Providence 1968

    Visions and Revisions. Museum of Art, Rhode Island School of Design, Providence, 1968.

Ragghianti Collobi 1974

    Ragghianti Collobi, Licia. *Il Libro di Disegni del Vasari.* 2 vols., Florence, 1974.

Rearick 1958

    Rearick, Walter R. "Battista Franco and the Grimani Chapel" *Saggi e memorie di storia dell'arte* 2 (1958-59), 107-139.

Redig de Campos

    Redig de Campos, Diocleccio. *I Palazzi Vaticani.* Rome, 1967.

Rome 1984

    Oltre Raffaello. Rome, (May-July), 1984.

Rutgers 1984

    Six Centuries of Art on Paper from the Ackland Art Museum. The Jane Voorhees Zimmerli Art Museum, Rutgers, State University of New Jersey, New Brunswick, 1984.

Ryskamp 1984

    Ryskamp, Charles, ed. *Twentieth Report to the Fellows of the Pierpont Morgan Library, 1981-1983.* New York, 1984.

Saint Louis 1970

    "Drawings by Federico Zuccaro and Sir Edward John Poynter." *City Art Museum of Saint Louis Bulletin* 6 (November-December 1970), 4-7.

Scholz 1967

    Scholz, Janos. "Italian Drawings in the Art Museum of Princeton University." *The Burlington Magazine* 109 (May 1967), 290-199.

Scholz 1976

    Scholz, Janos. *Italian Master Drawings 1350-1800 from the Janos Scholz Collections.* New York, 1976.

Schultz 1980

      Schultz, Juergen. "Tintoretto and the First Competition for the Ducal Palace 'Paradise'" *Arte Veneta* 34 (1980), 112-126.

Sinding-Larsen 1974

      Sinding-Larsen, S. "Christ in the Council Hall; Studies in the Religious Iconography of the Venetian Republic." *Acta ad Archaeologiam et Artium Historiam Pertinentia* Vol. 5, Rome, 1974.

Siren 1917

      Siren, Osvald. *Italienska handleckingar fra 1400 - och 1500 talen i Nationalmuseum.* Stockholm, 1917.

Smith 1970

      Smith, Graham. "A Drawing for the Interior Decoration of the Casino of Pius IV." *The Burlington Magazine* 112 (February 1970), 108-111.

Smith 1973

      Smith, Graham. "Two Drawings by Federico Barocci." *Bulletin of the Detroit Institute of the Arts* 52, nos. 2-3 (1973), 83-91.

Smith 1977

      Smith, Graham. *The Casino of Pius IV.* Princeton, 1977.

Smith 1978a

      Smith, Graham. "A Drawing by Federico Zuccaro for the *Last Judgment* in Florence Cathedral." *Bulletin*, Museums of Art and Archaeology, The University of Michigan 1 (1978), 27-41.

Smith 1978b

      Smith, Graham. "Federico Barocci at Cleveland and New Haven." *The Burlington Magazine* 120 (May 1978), 330-333.

Spiro and Coleman 1987

      Spiro, Stephen B. and Robert Randolf Coleman. *Master Drawings the Wisdom-Reilly Collection.* The Snite Museum of Art, The University of Notre Dame, 1987.

Staten Island 1958

      Italian Drawings and Sculpture from the Renaissance to the Present. Staten Island Museum, 1958-59.

Staten Island 1961

      Italian Drawings from the Janos Scholz Collection. Staten Island Museum.

Stechow 1976

      Stechow, Wolfgang. *Catalog of Drawings and Watercolors in the Allen Memorial Art Museum, Oberlin College.* Oberlin, 1976.

Stix and Fröhlich-Bum 1932

      Stix, A. and L. Fröhlich-Bum. *Beschreibender Katalog der Handzeichnungen in der graphischen Sammlung Albertina.* Vol. 3, Vienna, 1932.

Strinati 1974

      Strinati, Claudio. "Gli anni dificile di Federico Zuccari." *Storia dell'Arte* 21 (1974), 95-117.

Stubbe 1963

      Stubbe, Wolf. *Italienische Meisterzeichnungen vom 14 bis zum 18 Jahrhundert aus amerikanischem Besitz die Sammlung Janos Scholz.* Kunsthalle, Hamburg, 1963.

Szabó 1975

      Szabó, George. *The Robert Lehman Collection: A Guide.* The Metropolitan Museum of Art, New York, 1975.

Taylor 1976

      Taylor, Mary Cazort. *European Drawings from Canadian Collections.* The National

Gallery of Canada, Ottawa, 1976.

Tietze-Conrat 1940

Tietze-Conrat, Erica. "Decorative Paintings of the Venetian Renaissance Reconstructed from Drawings." *Art Quarterly* 3 (Winter 1940), 19ff.

Tokyo 1977

Renaissance Decorative Arts from the Robert Lehman Collection of the Metropolitan Museum of Art. The National Museum of Western Art, Tokyo, 1977.

Tokyo 1979

European Master Drawings of Six Centuries from the Collection of the Fogg Art Museum. The National Museum of Western Art, Tokyo, 1979.

Tolnay 1970

Tolnay, Charles de. "Il *Paradiso* del Tintoretto, Note sull'interpretazione della tela in Palazzo Ducale." *Arte Veneta* 24 (1970), 117ff.

Valconover 1960

Valconover, Francesco. *All the Paintings of Titian*. 2 vols. New York, 1960.

Van Gelder 1971

Van Gelder, J.G. "Jan de Bisschop." *Oud-Holland* 86 (1971), 201-288.

Van Mander 1973

Van Mander, Karel. *Den Grondt der edel vry schilder-const*. Hessel Miedema, ed. Utrecht, 1973.

Vasari 1850

Vasari, Giorgio. *Lives of the Most Eminent Painters, Sculptors and Architects*. translated by Mrs. Jonathan Foster, 5 vols., London, 1850-52.

Venice 1957

Venetian Drawings from the Scholz Collection. Fondazione Giorgio Cini, Venice, 1957.

Venturi

Venturi, Adolfo. *Storia dell' arte italiana*. vol. 9 Milan, 1925-34.

Vey 1958

Vey, Horst. *A Catalogue of Drawings by European Masters in the Worcester Art Museum*. Worcester, 1958.

Vitzthum 1954

Vitzthum, Walter. "Zuccaro's *Paradise* for the Doge's Palace." *The Burlington Magazine* 96 (September 1954), 291.

Vitzthum 1965

[Vitzthum, Walter]. "Review: Popham-Fenwick, *European Drawings in the Collection of the National Gallery of Canada*." *Master Drawings* 3 (Fall 1965), 409.

Vitzthum 1966

Vitzthum, Walter. "Publications received: *Mostra di disegni degli Zuccari*, Exhibition catalogue by John Gere." *Master Drawings* 4 (Fall 1966), 311-313.

Vitzthum 1969

Vitzthum, Walter. "Drawings from Stockholm." *Revue de l'art* 5 (1969), 93.

Vitzthum 1970

Vitzthum, Walter. *A Selection of Italian Drawings from North American Collections*. Norman Mackenzie Art Gallery, University of Saskatchewan, Regina, 1970.

Voss 1920

Voss, Hermann. *Die Malerei der Spätrenaissance in Röm und Florenz*. 2 vols., Leipzig, 1920.

Voss 1954

Voss, Hermann. "Project of Federico Zuccari for the *Paradise* in the Doge's Palace." *The*

Burlington Magazine 96 (June 1954), 172-175.

Ward 1984
Ward, Roger. Review of "Master Drawings from the Woodner Collection." *The Burlington Magazine* 126 (April 1984), 251.

Ward-Jackson 1979
Ward-Jackson, Peter. *Italian Drawings: Volume One, 14th-16th Centuries.* Department of Prints and Drawings, Victoria and Albert Museum, London, 1979.

Washington, D.C. 1974
National Gallery of Art, Recent Acquisitions and Promised Gifts, Sculpture, Drawings, Prints. Washington, D.C., 1974.

Washington, D.C. 1978
Master Drawings from the Collection of the National Gallery of Art and Promised Gifts. Washington, D.C., 1978.

Washington, D.C. 1988
Master Drawings from the National Gallery of Canada. National Gallery of Art, Washington, D.C., 1988.

Wegner 1984
Wegner, Susan E. "A Witness to the Raising of Lazarus, a Drawing by Federico Zuccaro." *Source Notes in the History of Art* 4 (Fall 1984), 7-11.

Weiner 1985
Mia N. Weiner Presents an Exhibition of Old Master Drawings. Piero Corsini, Inc., New York, 1985.

Winner 1962
Winner, Matthias. "Gemalte Kunsttheorie." *Jahrbuch der Berliner Museen,* n.f., 4 (1962), 172ff.

Zeri 1957
Zeri, Federico. *Pittura e contrariforma: l'arte senza tempo di Scipione da Gaeta.* Turin, 1957.

Zuccari
Zuccari, Federico. *Il Passaggio per l'Italia con la dimora di Parma.* ed. Lanciarini. Rome, 1893.

PHOTOGRAPHS

Ackland Art Museum, University of North Carolina at Chapel Hill, no. 47; Marcello Aldega/Margot Gordon, New York, no. 49; Alinari/ Art Resource, New York, figs. 10, 12, 21, 36, 43, 47; Allen Memorial Art Museum, Oberlin College, no. 41; Art Gallery of Ontario, Toronto, no. 10; The Art Institute of Chicago, nos. 15, 30, 69, 90; Ashmolean Museum, Oxford, fig. 5; The Art Museum, Princeton University, nos. 4, 17, 50, 92, 101; The Baltimore Museum of Art, nos. 20, 80; William Botman & Son, Montreal, no. 58; Brigdens, Regina, no. 43; The Cleveland Museum of Art, no. 14; A.C. Cooper, Christie's, nos. 1, 40, 42, 63, figs. 20, 39; Cooper-Hewitt Museum, The Smithsonian Institution's National Institute of Design, New York, nos. 9, 12, 93; Christ Church, Oxford, fig. 41; Christie, Manson and Woods, no. 60; Prudence Cumming, fig. 44; Duke Roberto Ferretti, nos. 45, 82; Fogg Art Museum, Harvard University, Cambridge, Massachusetts, nos. 13, 25, 31, 67, 81, fig. 30; Lynton Gardiner, New York, nos. 7, 89; The J. Paul Getty Museum, Malibu, nos. 36, 87, 98; Stanley Greenberg, no. 74: Andrew Harkins, no. 75; Istituto Centrale per il Catalogo e la Documentazione, Rome, figs. 4, 6, 7, 11, 13-15, 18, 27, 35; Jak Katalan, no. 95.; Los Angeles County Museum of Art, no. 39; The Metropolitan Museum of Art, New York, nos. 5, 16, 19, 27, 28, 48, 57, 61, 66, 84, figs. 28, 29, 45; Alfred Moir Collection, no. 83; Museum of Fine Arts, Boston, nos. 55, 76, fig. 26; National Gallery of Art, Washington, D.C., nos. 11, 62, 64; National Gallery of Canada, Ottawa, nos. 23, 70, 94; The Nelson-Atkins Museum of Art, Kansas City, no. 77; The Philadelphia Museum of Art, nos. 33, 75; The Pierpont Morgan Library, New York, nos. 22, 26, 34, 35, 38, 53, 54, 78, 79, 85, 86, 97, 100; The Rosenbach Museum and Library, Philadelphia, no. 73; The Saint Louis Art Museum, no. 65; The Snite Museum of Art, University of Notre Dame, nos. 24, 59, 91; Soprint. per i Beni Ambient. e Architettonici del Lazio, Rome, figs. 1, 3; Sotheby's, no. 37, figs. 16, 25, 31, 33, 38, 42, 45; Staatliche Graphische Sammlung, Munich, fig. 19; Staatliche Museen zu Berlin, East Berlin, fig. 2; David Stansbury, no. 8; University Art Museum, University of California, Santa Barbara, no. 102; The University of Michigan Museum of Art, Ann Arbor, no. 32; Vasari, Rome, figs. 37, 40, 46; Vatican Museums, figs. 9, 22, 23, 24; Wallace Collection, London, fig. 8; Graydon Wood, no. 44; Worcester Art Museum, no. 103; Yale University Art Gallery, New Haven, nos. 3 (Richard Caspole), 52, 56 (Joseph Szazfal), 68, 104